The Dra

CLASSIC ENGLISH SHORT STORIES

Oxford New York
OXFORD UNIVERSITY PRESS
1988

Oxford University Press, Walton Street, Oxford OX2 6DP
Oxford New York Toronto
Delhi Bombay Calcutta Madras Karachi
Petaling Jaya Singapore Hong Kong Tokyo
Nairobi Dar es Salaam Cape Town
Melbourne Auckland

and associated companies in
Beirut Berlin Ibadan Nicosia

Oxford is a trade mark of Oxford University Press

First published as English Short Stories of Today *1939*
First issued, with the title The Dragon's Head, *as an*
Oxford University Press paperback 1988

British Library Cataloguing in Publication Data
[English short stories of today]
The dragon's head: classic English
short stories.
823'.01'08
ISBN 0–19–282148–2

Library of Congress Cataloging in Publication Data
English short stories of to-day.
The dragon's head.
Previously published as: English short stories of
to-day. 1939.
1. Short stories, English. 2. English fiction—
20th century. I. Oxford University Press. II. Title.
PR1309.S5E53 1988 823'01'08 87–31413
ISBN 0–19–282148–2 (pbk.)

Printed in Great Britain by
The Guernsey Press Co. Ltd.
Guernsey, Channel Islands

PREFACE

THE short story, in one form or another, is of such extreme antiquity that its history may be said to begin before that of literature itself. Here was the natural vehicle for folk-lore and fable, the mould in which the legendary lore of all primitive races tended to harden. What admirable raw material Greek mythology offered to tellers of brief tales in verse or prose was perceived in due course by such Roman writers as Ovid and Apuleius, but long before that time the Chinese, the Egyptians, and the authors of some of the apocryphal books of the Bible had produced masterpieces in this kind.

An immense stream of stories, fed by tributaries from India, Persia, and Araby, moved westward during the Middle Ages and overflowed into the writings of Boccaccio, Chaucer, and the nameless compilers of such collections as the *Cente Novelle Antiche* and the *C Mery Talys.* By the end of the fourteenth century the short story had already fallen into its four main categories, the realistic, the humorous, the romantic, and the allegorical. Then, as now, affinity was closest between humour and realism, and incompatibility greatest between realism and romance. Allegory, which does not concern us much (though it seems to be struggling to get its second wind in modern symbolism) was at one time a very fruitful parent of the short story.

In one way or another the form retained its hold upon popular taste, if not upon academic favour; and even the Age of Reason, usually so inimical to brevity, could not wholly disregard it. English novelists like Fielding, who introduced short stories into the framework of their long novels, were imitated in a later age by Scott, whose 'Wandering Willie's Tale' (in *Redgauntlet*) is as good as anything of its kind is likely ever to be, and by Dickens, who in the early stages of his development seemed as if he were going to carry on the tradition. But the Victorian period preferred its fiction, like its gentlemen's beards and its ladies' dresses, to be long and copious, and, in spite of the excellent work done by Lytton, Le Fanu, and others, the short story languished in England, though it flourished in America and in France.

In the closing decades of the nineteenth and the opening years of the twentieth century a group of English writers, among whom were R. L. Stevenson, Henry James, Oscar Wilde, and Rudyard Kipling, turned their attention, with almost startling and certainly excellent results, to this somewhat neglected literary medium.

A restless and impatient age took kindly to the short story. It has never lost its hold and, while keeping more or less within its ancient lines of demarcation, it has subdued unto itself many things of which its earlier exponents recked nothing.

Far more than poetry, which has its own universality of time as well as of place, this prose-form has shown, and still shows, 'the very age and body of the time, his form and pressure'. It is thus of importance to the student of social conditions, of intellectual movements, and of historical perspective, as well as to the student of literature pure and simple.

CONTENTS

STELLA BENSON

On the Contrary

LEONARD LUMLEY had some very good ideas for keeping cool in the Red Sea. 'Wear *wool* next the skin,' he said, 'and drink nothing but very hot tea. . . .' He had many such ideas, but no one could be absolutely certain that he practised what he preached. Hot tea was not served, for instance, in the bar, where Leonard spent a good deal of his time, and it seemed that he had lost his only collar-stud, so that his shirt-collar flapped open in defiance of his dictum that Closed Collars were Coolest. However, the very contrariness of his views was impressive, and Leonard himself was a very impressive, though rather stout, young man. Several people trusted him so much that they went about for a day or two in thick Jaegers, looking like kettles boiling over. Miss Dancey admired him so much that she must have lost several pints in weight between Suez and Perim.

Leonard, instinctively aware that all that he could say was safe in Miss Dancey's ear, sat very often at the foot of her deck-chair—indeed partly *on* her feet, since he was of spreading figure—but spiritually, as he knew, their positions were reversed! *His* were the feet that were sat at. He believed that every man should have a profession, he would tell her—but not before he is forty. A man should afford himself leisure while he is young and work when he is old.

'Oh—*oh*, what an eggstrawdinarily interesting idea,' said Miss Dancey.

Leisure is only useful to the young, according to

Leonard Lumley; after forty a man should begin to work, having nothing better to do, and should work harder and harder until the age of ninety or so, when death, the supremely full-time job, should interrupt him at his desk or in the pulpit or on his charger riding into battle or at his stethoscope or what not. For, though Mr. Lumley was just over thirty-five and would soon come to the end of his period of leisure, he had not yet decided on the occupation that would most fruitfully employ his declining years.

'Oh—*oh*—a *doctor*,' suggested Miss Dancey. 'Doctors are *magnificent*, I think—perfect *saints*. . . .'

'On the contrary,' said Leonard, to whose lips this phrase rose almost automatically. 'The doctor's profession is the least noble of any. A stockbroker is more saintly than a doctor.'

'Oh—*oh*—not *really*—do, *do* tell me why. . . .'

'Well, it's to a doctor's interest, you must remember, to live in a sickly world, and also—er—well, if you knew as much about doctors and stockbrokers as I do. . . .'

'Oh—*oh*—' breathed Miss Dancey. 'Then *why* not be a *stockbroker*? Then you'd be both *rich* and *saintly*. . . .'

'On the contrary,' replied Leonard. 'Stockbrokers never make money. Not a penny. They always die in the workhouse.'

'Oh—*oh*—how eggstrawdinary that is. . . . Can you *explain* it to me?'

'Well, you can take it from me,' said Leonard. And she did. Stockbrokers and doctors being thus thrust beyond the pale, she tried soldiers, clergymen, barristers . . . imagining herself the wife of each in turn. But all, it seemed, were not only unsuitable but impossible; soldiers were slaves, clergymen's inhibitions invariably landed them in lunatic asylums, barristers, being always corrupt, finished up in jail.

'*Sailors*, then,' whispered Miss Dancey, a trifle discouraged. 'Such *breezy*, *healthy darlings*, sailors. . . .'

'On the contrary,' said Leonard. 'I can always see in a sailor's eye that introspective, scarcely sane look that tells of a life spent within unnaturally narrow limits. Show me a sailor and I'll show you a potential homicidal hysteric.'

'Oh, Lord!' said a voice near them.

Leonard looked round, annoyed, to see who this might be that so impertinently appealed from his authority to a Higher Power. He saw Mr. Hospice, s.s. *Meritoria*'s third officer, pausing in a walk round the deck with some unknown fellow-homicidal-hysteric of minor rank.

'Oh—*oh*—Mr. Hospice,' said Miss Dancey. 'I'm learning *such* a *lot* of new things.' (There had been a difference of opinion among the passengers as to whether Miss Dancey ever intended sarcasm. Fortunately for her popularity, however, it was finally proved that she never did.)

'Thplendid,' said Mr. Hospice. 'Thorry I interrupted. I couldn't help overhearing Mithter Lumley'th latht remark, and it thurprithed me rather. Thorry.' And he and his friend strode away down the deck.

Mr. Lumley, who whole-heartedly despised the thin undersized third officer, was beginning to tell Miss Dancey how perfect an example was this Hospice of all the Lumley theories—when—something happened.

Really, for the first two or three minutes, the passengers could hardly tell what had happened. It was like an earthquake reversed—a sort of lurch from regular movement into stillness. It had the same deeply disturbing effect on the nerves as has an earthquake—gave feet that had learned to trust their foothold a sense of betrayal. The ship, after a futile churning of propellers, was motionless, but listed very slightly. Passengers streamed out of the smoking-room, to ask Leonard what had happened.

The moonlight, which had long been exhibiting a silver panorama of sea to no audience, now attracted general attention. Everybody crowded to the rail, trying, with anxious gimlet eyes, to bore through the curiously substantial silvered air. Every one expected to see—what? A rock? A whale? Some unthinkable menace? Something, at any rate, to write to one's horrified family about from Colombo. Perhaps, even, something that would get into the papers and enable them all to be called Survivors. But there was nothing to be seen except calm sea and, a mile or so away—by the very keen-sighted—very low unobtrusive land.

'*Don't* look over the rail,' rang Leonard's commanding voice. 'In danger, the best thing is *not* to know the worst. Now I propose we all sit down on the deck and play some silly game like Old Maid or something. Better than singing "Nearer My God to Thee", what?'

'Oh—*oh*,' quavered Miss Dancey. 'Then there really *is* danger?'

'Who's got playing-cards on the spot?' asked Leonard. 'Hi, don't go mooning over the rail there, I tell you. Turn your eyes inboard, everybody, and remember you're English.'

'Oh—*oh*—is there anything very *terrible* to be seen over the rail?' asked Miss Dancey hoarsely.

'Cards—cards—cards,' called Leonard gaily.

'Yipp-i-yaddy,' echoed Mr. Hospice, appearing from the direction of the bridge. 'We're aground.'

'Don't make such a fuss, man,' said Leonard sharply. 'You—an officer—ought to know better than to frighten the ladies like that. But we're not going to be frightened, are we?' he added, looking lovingly at his flock—of which Miss Dancey was the bell-wether. 'Not a bit frightened. We're going to play Old Maid sitting on the deck. What a lark!'

'Oh, for the Lord'th thake, don't be tho dam *brave*,' said Mr. Hospice in a low voice. He added more loudly, 'We're aground—on thand—till high tide to-morrow morning. No danger whatever.'

Only a dread of being ridiculous restrained Leonard from strangling Mr. Hospice on the spot. For, unfortunately for the landsman, words spoken from above the brassy buttons of a uniform had a completely soothing effect on the listeners. Nobody even dreamed of playing Old Maid. Everybody went back to interrupted bridge and poker. Everybody in due course went to bed and to sleep—though every one kept, as it were, one ear awake for the sound of a change in the ship's condition.

There was no change. Promenaders before breakfast saw still the same sluggish sea, the same sullen low land. Even the jellyfish looked as if they had been there for generations. Leonard was, by the mercy of his gods, enabled to say at breakfast, 'I told you so. . . . Off at high tide indeed. . . . Didn't I *say* that little shrimp of a third officer didn't know his job?'

Meeting Mr. Hospice on deck after breakfast, he said acidly, 'In spite of your hopeful promise, Mr. Hospice, we're still aground.'

'Why, by jove—*tho* we are!' exclaimed Mr. Hospice blithely.

Leonard had no shyness of asking captains questions. The bluff and buttony spotlessness of captains imposed no humility on him. He felt himself the *moral* captain of every ship he travelled in. Actual captains were sometimes a little irritated by his assumption of a constant right to claim *tête-à-têtes* with them, but Leonard never observed this irritation. The captain of the *Meritoria* admitted, a little fretfully, on being buttonholed by Leonard, that the ship of which they shared the command had taken a firmer seat on the sand than had at first been supposed. 'It'll be a matter of shifting cargo,' said the captain, as he abruptly took flight.

'It'll be a matter of shifting cargo,' retailed Leonard to his flock on deck. 'We shall be here—oh . . . er . . . well . . . quite a time. . . .'

'Oh—*oh*—quite a *time*?' echoed Miss Dancey. 'What would happen if the sea got rough? The ship would break up. Like in *Robinson Crusoe*.'

'On the contrary,' said Leonard. 'The waves would help to jerk us off—but that's a technical question and I won't go into it now. The—er—south-west typhoon isn't due at this time of year. . . .' Even his hopeful ear detected a flaw in his omniscience here, so he changed the subject. 'What do you all say to my suggestion to the captain that we passengers go ashore for the day? Just to get out of the way while they're shifting cargo.'

'It would be dam hot,' said Bertie Briggs, a slightly mutinous male lamb of his flock, looking at the scarred, heat-dazzled line of land.

'On the contrary,' said Leonard. 'It would be far cooler than in the ship. I've spent years of my life in the tropics and you can take it from me that the way to keep cool in a hot climate is to *keep out* of whatever breeze there is. Directly I take over a house in India, I immediately scrap all punkahs and electric fans. Immediately. "Take the beastly things away," I say to the servants. "I'm not going to sit and catch pneumonia under those fancy gadgets like a callow tourist. . . ."'

A callow tourist! Every tourist within earshot shuddered, shocked at such an idea. For a tourist to behave like a tourist—how degrading! About twenty tourist passengers felt obliged to disprove their shameful touristhood by consenting to an expedition to the windless shore, if it could be arranged.

Leonard and Miss Dancey had some difficulty in finding the captain. 'These sailors simply don't know their job,' he said to her as they followed rumours of the captain all over the ship. 'Look at this so-called captain—gets his ship into a hole like this, and then disappears—can't be found, it seems, by any of his subordinates. Why, anything might happen—and yet nobody knows where to lay their hands on the man supposed to be responsible.'

'Oh—*oh—might* anything happen?'

They finally ran the captain to earth in the chartroom. 'I'm afraid, Miss Dancey, I can't invite passengers to come and see me here——' he began, but Leonard managed, by talking in a very loud voice, to explain the object of their visit. The captain's attention was caught. 'Well,' he said, on a note of hope, 'I can't think why you should want to go to a burnt-up hole like that, but if you *do* want to—far be it from me. . . . We shall probably spend the day shifting cargo and get off at high tide early to-morrow. You going too, little Miss Dancey? Well, ladies do certainly have some odd fancies. I'll send my third officer, Mr. Hospice, to undertake the expedition.'

'Oh, I'll undertake the expedition all right, captain,' said Leonard.

'God help it, I know you will,' replied the captain with unexpected vigour. 'Let's say, then, that Mr. Hospice will *over*take the *under*taker. . . . Ha-ha. He'll have the boat ready in half an hour's time. I'm afraid I'm busy now. Good-bye. Enjoy yourselves.'

'All ships' captains suffer from a superiority complex,' said Leonard, looking a little ruffled as he helped Miss Dancey down the companion-way. 'They seem to think their authority is supreme.'

'Oh—*oh*—*so* they do. . . . But *isn't* it—on board their own ship?'

'On the contrary. In these days of trade unions, the captain is the slave of the humblest stoker on board.'

'Oh—*oh*—*really*? Then oughtn't we to have gone and asked the humblest stoker on board if we might . . .?'

Really Miss Dancey was almost silly sometimes, thought Leonard.

However, as the boat, bristling with twenty passengers, was rowed to shore, he felt the joy of creation and domination—even though Mr. Hospice was ostensibly in charge—for certainly no other than Leonard Lumley had led out these bleating Israelites from their Egypt—had set the strong machinery of these rowing Lascars' arms in motion.

The most beautiful moment of the expedition was the moment of landing. As the wrinkled sea-bottom, sloping lightly upwards under blue space, stopped being sea-bottom and became Arabia—as the keel of the boat gently grooved the ochre sand, it seemed to all the adventurers that they were about to do something wholly new for the first time. In marking that dazzling virgin beach with their feet, they would print some mystic and undreamt-of word on the only really blank page their eyes had ever rested on. One by one they jumped out of their boat, murmuring or shrilling their astonishment. The shore—the whole land as far as eye could see—seemed to be newly created by some brusque movement of the earth, like a great nut newly cracked in haphazard fragments. Jagged rocks lay lightly on the sand; nothing was embedded or rooted. The very vegetation was only laid on the sand's surface in the form of large round rolling transparencies of dried tangled shrub—like ogres' thistledowns blown from far roots by some dusty long-dead wind. The uncouth newly-broken rocks were sparsely scattered about the shore, were grouped into a crazy Stonehenge just about high-water mark, and, a little farther inland still, were built into a long ridge which had acted as a kind of dam for the low-blown, shifting, sifting sand from the desert. The horizon, therefore, was very close. The Magnificent Infinities which Leonard had promised his flock were shut away by this wave of rock and sand.

'Oh—*oh*——,' cried Miss Dancey. 'How eggstrawdinarily eggciting it all is. So *dangerous*-looking, kind of. I believe I saw a man's head behind that rock. I suppose this country is *crammed* with *sheiks*.'

'On the contrary,' said Leonard. 'You may take it from me that there isn't a living soul within three hundred miles.'

As he spoke, a young dark boy, almost naked, stepped out from behind a rock where he had been hiding to watch the landing of the strangers.

'—Except, of course,' added Leonard with some presence of mind, 'a few fisher families scattered along the coast.'

'I suppose they're practically savages,' said elderly Mrs. Wilkins, looking dubiously at the morose child.

'On the contrary. Like all simple peoples, they are extremely friendly. They haven't learned to distrust strangers.' He held out his hand with a coin in it. The simple boy seized a rock and threw it at the group—fortunately unskilfully—before he ran away shouting something that, one feared, was an Arabian curse.

'Well, well,' said Leonard, 'boys will be boys all the world over. Now, everybody—let's *enjoy* ourselves. . . . Isn't it *good* to feel the solid earth under our feet again?'

'Yes *and* no,' said Mr. Briggs rather impudently. 'The solid earth is almost burning the soles off my shoes. If you'd told me what we were in for, I'd have brought a pair of stilts along. What's the next move?'

'*My* next move is into the shade of that pile of rocks,' said Mrs. Wilkins, who was rather stout. 'It must be cooler there.'

'On the contrary. . . .' But Leonard's flock, showing a disquieting independence, moved away from him as one lamb, towards the strip of red quivering shadow.

'We'd better have our cool drinkth now or never,' said Mr. Hospice, who had been superintending two cross-looking stewards in the removal of several hampers into the shade. 'The ithed lemonade'll be hot toddy thoon.'

'I strongly disapprove of iced drinks in hot weather,' began Leonard. 'I have often——'

'Oh, thplendid,' said Mr. Hospice. 'Tho much more for the retht of uth.'

There was nothing for Leonard to do but to follow

the party to the strip of shade. It was a narrow strip, growing narrower, and they were obliged to sit in a long row to enjoy it. The sand here certainly felt cool in contrast to the baked shore. Mrs. Wilkins said, 'Really, this is quite pleasant,' in a tone of surprise.

'Yes *and* no,' grumbled Mr. Briggs, for at that moment the flies discovered the party.

'I wonder how long we can thtick thith out,' said Mr. Hospice cheerfully.

Nobody answered, but every one—even Leonard—silently wished that it would not seem ridiculous to leave Arabia after a visit of only nine minutes.

'Oh—*oh*—it's an *adventure*, anyway,' said Miss Dancey.

'On the contrary. It is a popular fallacy that adventure is found in wild remote places like this. You can take it from me that there is more chance of adventure in the Strand, London, than in the whole of the Arabian desert.'

His luck seemed to be out to-day, for as he finished speaking a startling adventure began happening to them, that certainly would have been unlikely in the Strand. A torrent of dirty and wild-looking men began streaming round from behind the ridge of rocks against which they sat. All were shouting—not apparently to any one in particular—and each carried a naked dagger or a kind of a billhook. They came and stood in front of the long line of seated picnickers—and continued coming—more and more of them—until the travellers' view of the sea was completely shut out. The heat and smell, within this human stockade, became almost unbearable.

'My hat,' said Mr. Hospice, standing up. 'Thethe beggarth don't look any too friendly.'

'On the contrary,' said Leonard, 'they are no doubt

friendly fishcrfolk, inviting us to visit their village. I see evidences of native industries. Look at the coloured plaited leather round the hilts of their weapons.'

'Look at their toes,' said Bertie Briggs. 'All eaten away.'

Their feet were the easiest part of them to look at, since all the lookers were seated. To stand up against the overhanging boulders, one would have to stand almost nose to nose with the visitors.

'I don't want to look at anything,' said Mrs. Wilkins. 'I shall be sick in a minute.'

Since Mr. Hospice was standing, the Arabs made the mistake of supposing that he was the travellers' mouthpiece, especially as he spoke a little Arabic. So Leonard sat back trying to smile subtly, like a general leaving the drudgery to his aide-de-camp.

'Well, well,' said Mr. Hospice, after a long bellowing talk with the head man, who wore red and sandy striped draperies. 'It theemth thethe beggarth want thome of our good money off uth. No leth than twenty poundth, in fact.'

'Whatever for?' asked Mrs. Wilkins, letting go of her nose for the purpose.

'Well, thtrangely enough, for the privilege of going back on board.'

'Oh—*oh*—are they brigands?' asked Miss Dancey.

'Thomething like it, I'm afraid. But we're perfectly thafe, really. Only I thuppothe there'th nothing for it but to pay up.'

'On the contrary,' began Leonard, but Mr. Briggs interrupted him, 'Can't we knock some of 'em down and run for it? They've got no fire-arms.'

'Oh—*oh*—*don't* talk like that. . . . I'm going to faint,'

cried Miss Dancey, and she certainly began to cant alarmingly towards Leonard's shoulder.

'I've got eight and sixpence,' said a desiccated Major. Apart from this sum, no one had more than a shilling or so.

'Well, talk—talk, my dear fellow,' said Leonard to Mr. Hospice. 'Talk, to gain time while I think out a plan of action. *Bargain* with the brutes. Bargaining is the essence of Oriental business.'

'Very pothibly it ith,' agreed Mr. Hospice. 'I've been bargaining like hell. They athked forty firtht—they now conthent to take twenty. No amount of bargaining'll bring 'em down from twenty poundth to theventeen and thixpenthe—which ith all we've got.'

'Let *me* talk to them,' said Leonard, heaving himself to his feet among the crowding draperies of the Arabs. They began laughing coarsely, for some obscure reason expecting entertainment. 'Now then, you scoundrels,' he shouted authoritatively. But he stopped because a lean black hand darted forward and removed his pince-nez from his nose, snapping the little chain that tethered them to his bosom. 'Here—I say—drop it—this is too much—this is robbery.'

But the pince-nez were by now straddling a broad black nose at least twenty noses away from their owner's.

'Better rethign ourthelveth, I'm afraid,' said Mr. Hospice. 'They want me to go back to the ship and get the money, and I think I'd better, on the whole. You'll be quite thafe, ath long ath you don't annoy them. You're *money* to them.'

'So damned ignominious,' said Mr. Briggs.

But Leonard did not feel ignominious, though his eyes, without their glasses, had rather a pink wincing look.

'Yes, go back,' he said haughtily, 'and ask the captain from me to send a party of armed men—all the arms he has, and——'

But Mr. Hospice was hurrying down the beach to where the Lascars—all agog—were waiting in the boat.

'I'd like to see the captain's face when he gets my message,' said Leonard, looking down his line of wilting followers. 'He'll agree with me, of course, that an armed demonstration would be a better course than tamely paying up.'

'Oh—*oh*——' wailed Miss Dancey. 'But if these brigands see men with guns coming, they'll cut our throats—I'm sure of it. They've got us so squeezed up against this cliff.'

'On the contrary,' said Leonard. 'We have a strategic position. An Englishman with his back to the wall is the toughest man to beat on God's earth, you can take it from me.'

'Oh—*oh*—you're so *brave*. . . . I wish I was *brave*. . . .'

'I wish I had a severe cold in the head,' said Mrs. Wilkins.

Now that Mr. Hospice was gone, the robbers seemed to recognize Leonard's leadership, though in no very flattering way. They made him the butt of their simple wit, as he stood among them, trying to trip him up with their sinuous black feet, pushing his hat over his nose, tweaking his coat, putting their hands in his pockets, and even trying to pinch his ear. From above, a shaggy head looking over a split boulder—like holly on the top of a partly eaten plum-pudding—was engaged in spitting assiduously down on to the captives. Leonard haughtily moved out of the range of this marksman.

'Better stand in the shade, Lumley,' said the Major.

'You're the only one of us without a topee or a sunshade.'

'On the contrary,' said Leonard grimly. 'The topee is the cause of more cases of sunstroke than . . . you can take it from me. . . . Oh, *when* is this blasted little sailor coming back? The inefficiency of sailors is simply——' He covered his burst of petulance with—'I'm longing to have a dozen armed men behind me and put these damned niggers in their places. . . . Excuse my language, ladies.'

'Oh—*oh*—you are so *brave*. . . .'

'I can see a boat—no, *two* boats, leaving the ship now,' said Mr. Briggs.

'Two boats—that means forty men,' said Leonard. 'I knew the captain would agree with me. Pay up, indeed—what nonsense!'

There was a pause and then Mr. Briggs said, 'The boats are empty, except for Hospice and the men rowing.'

'On the contrary,' said Leonard, 'the armed men are all crouching out of sight. Even Hospice would have too much sense to show his hand too soon.'

'The two boats are separating now,' continued Mr. Briggs. 'One's going to land right away down the beach. Very mysterious.'

'Not in the least,' said Leonard. 'They understood my suggestions perfectly. Lord, I wish I could get my glasses back so that I could see the fun.'

But there was no fun to see. The two boats ran ashore about a hundred yards apart, and Mr. Hospice alone jumped out of the nearest one. Even the robbers listened as he began shouting. His voice reached his friends across the hot air with a brittle, almost microphonic sound. 'I'm going to walk thlowly up the beach while you walk thlowly down to that farther boat. I'll thet the pathe. You mutht all be thafe in the boat by the time I reach the niggerth.'

'Must! Must!' exclaimed Leonard furiously. 'What does he mean—*must*? Are we to trot about the beach at his orders like a flock of sheep? I shan't move a step.'

'Well, I shall,' said the Major. 'And I advise the ladies. . . .'

But the ladies needed no advice; they were already gingerly filing between the bars of their living prison. A few robbers walked with them, shuffling along packed closely against their victims, treading on their heels, nudging their ribs, thrusting their chins into their back hair—meaning no harm, but impelled to this almost lover-like contiguity by their naïve curiosity.

'Not too fatht,' shrilled Mr. Hospice. 'Keep all together, and watch me.' He shouted in pidgin Arabic to the robbers. A group of them left the picnickers and started to meet him, but he at once retreated towards the boat. The Arabs, understanding the position, stood still, watching their victims receding, their reward approaching. Leonard stood sullenly against the rock, wondering what gesture of valour and authority remained to him to make.

'Oh—*oh*—Mr. Lumley,' Miss Dancey called back. '*Don't* stay there by yourself. . . . You'll be *killed*.'

'I must stand by Hospice,' said Leonard. This idea occurred to him one second before he put it into words.

The retreat and approach, regulated to synchronize, were slow, but at last the picnickers were safe in the boat and Mr. Hospice reached the robber group.

'Good Lord, Mithter Lumley—you thtill here? Why didn't you go with the otherth?'

'Because I'm a man and not a sheep.'

Mr. Hospice said nothing! He was counting out money into the chief robber's hand. All the Arabs wanted to look at the money; they craned and tiptoed behind each other like excited children. Leonard stood outside the group, trying to keep his looks in keeping with his latest gesture—'Standing By a Fellow Man.' The robbers, finding themselves all bowed by curiosity and avarice to one centre, suddenly awoke to the fact that in the messenger they had another hostage. Why not send Leonard back to the ship for another twenty pounds ransom? And then seize Leonard and send the sailor. What a delightfully easy way of making money, thought the simple fellows. Holding Mr. Hospice by every outlying fold in his clothes, they expounded their idea to him, pointing vigorously to Leonard. But just as Leonard was wondering what this (probably flattering) attention meant, Mr. Hospice, lithe as a fish, burst himself out of his clawed-at coat and kicked the robber chief in the stomach.

'Run for it, Lumley,' he shrieked—and ran.

Mr. Leonard Lumley's legs ran after him, bearing his reluctant body which still throbbed with the thought—'An Englishman never turns his back on danger.' Luckily, his legs knew better. They had never run so fast since they had had the honour of carrying Leonard.

A few of the Arabs, rather half-heartedly, pursued the fugitives, but most of them at once relinquished their too complex plan of seizing alternate hostages and earning ransom after ransom to infinity. They had had a remunerative morning's work, after all. Some of them came, shouting uncertainly, to the sea's edge, but Mr. Hospice and Leonard were being rowed swiftly away.

The picnickers were already safe on board the *Meritoria*.

'I thought there'd be trouble,' panted Leonard. 'As it turned out, I was quite right to stay and back you up.'

'Very noble of you, I'm thure.'

'I can't imagine why you didn't bring back a few guns and men as I told you to.'

'My dear thir, thothe bruteth would have cut all your throatth at the firtht shot. They had you penned up like pigth in a thty. Twenty poundth for the lot of you wath only a pound apiethe, after all. Worth that, to get free without bloodshed. Tho the Thkipper thought, at leatht.'

'Pigs in a sty.' Leonard was struck dumb by the outrageous description. What a detestable young man this was! He little knew that the kind Mr. Hospice was suppressing the captain's actual message—'Can't you arrange to pay up nineteen pounds nineteen shillings and elevenpence—and let 'em keep that dam-fool Lumley?'

Leonard and Mr. Hospice, on the deck of the *Meritoria*, found themselves the centre of a frenzied group of ex-picnickers and their friends. 'Oh—*oh*—OH—*what* an adventure.'

'On the contrary——' began Leonard—but his world suddenly played him false. It wavered, whirled, slipped upward, crashed, as he fell flat on the deck in the midst of his flock. Before he became quite unconscious, he heard two voices—good and evil—like the voices described by poets as A Voice and Another Voice.

'Oh—*oh*—poor *darling* Mr. Lumley—he's been so *wonderful*. . . .'

'Sunstroke. That's what comes of being such a —— fool as not to wear a topee. . . .'

'On the contrary,' gargled Leonard—but he was

obliged to reserve his retort for several days. And by that time it was not necessary, for Leonard's convalescence was brightened by the discovery that it was the intention of his flock to present him with a solid silver cigarette-case, in recognition of his splendid behaviour and competent leadership in the hour of danger. Even Mr. Hospice was to be given a pair of enamel cuff-links.

JOHN GALSWORTHY

Spindleberries

THE celebrated painter, Scudamore—whose studies of Nature had been hung on the line for so many years that he had forgotten the days when, not yet in the Scudamore manner, they depended from the sky—stood where his cousin had left him so abruptly. His lips, between comely grey moustache and comely pointed beard, wore a mortified smile, and he gazed rather dazedly at the spindleberries fallen on to the flagged courtyard from the branch she had brought to show him. Why had she thrown up her head as if he had struck her, and whisked round so that those dull-pink berries quivered and lost their rain-drops, and four had fallen? He had but said: 'Charming! I'd like to use them!' And she had answered: 'God!' and rushed away. Alicia really was crazed; who would have thought that once she had been so adorable? He stooped and picked up the four berries—a beautiful colour, that dull pink! And from below the coatings of success and the Scudamore manner a little thrill came up; the stir of emotional vision. Paint! What good? How express? He went across to the low wall which divided the courtyard of his expensively restored and beautiful old house from the first flood of the River Arun wandering silvery in pale winter sunlight. Yes, indeed! How express Nature, its translucence and mysterious unities, its mood never the same from hour to hour? Those brown-tufted rushes over there against the gold grey of light and water—those restless, hovering, white gulls. A kind of disgust at his own celebrated manner welled up within him—the disgust expressed in Alicia's 'God!' Beauty! What use—how express it? Had she been thinking the same thing?

He looked at the four pink berries glistening on the grey stone of the wall and memory stirred. What a lovely girl she had been, with her grey-green eyes shining under long lashes, the rose-petal colour in her cheeks, and the too-fine dark hair—now so very grey—always blowing a little wild. An enchanting, enthusiastic creature! He remembered, as if it had been but last week, that day when they started from Arundel Station by the road to Burpham, when he was twenty-nine and she twenty-five, both of them painters and neither of them famed—a day of showers and sunlight in the middle of March, and Nature preparing for full spring! How they had chattered at first; and when their arms touched, how he had thrilled, and the colour had deepened in her rain-wet cheeks; and then, gradually, they had grown silent; a wonderful walk, which seemed leading so surely to a more wonderful end. They had wandered round through the village and down past the chalk-pit and Jacob's ladder, into the field path and so to the river bank. And he had taken her ever so gently round the waist, still silent, waiting for that moment when his heart would leap out of him in words and hers—he was sure—would leap to meet it. The path entered a thicket of blackthorn with a few primroses close to the little river running full and gentle. The last drops of a shower were falling, but the sun had burst through, and the sky above the thicket was cleared to the blue of speedwell flowers. Suddenly she had stopped and cried: 'Look, Dick! Oh, look! It's heaven!' A high bush of blackthorn was lifted there, starry white against the blue and that bright cloud.

It seemed to sing, it was so lovely; the whole of spring was in it. But the sight of her ecstatic face had broken down all his restraint, and tightening his arm round her he had kissed her lips. He remembered still the expression of her face, like a child's startled out of sleep. She had gone rigid, gasped, started away from him, quivered and gulped, and broken suddenly into sobs. Then, slipping from his arm, she had fled. He had stood at first, amazed and hurt, utterly bewildered; then, recovering a little, had hunted for her full half an hour before at last he found her sitting on wet grass, with a stony look on her face. He had said nothing, and she nothing, except to murmur: 'Let's go on; we shall miss our train!' And all the rest of that day and the day after, until they parted, he had suffered from the feeling of having tumbled down off some high perch in her estimation. He had not liked it at all; it had made him very angry. Never from that day to this had he thought of it as anything but a piece of wanton prudery. Had it—had it been something else?

He looked at the four pink berries, and, as if they had uncanny power to turn the wheel of memory, he saw another vision of his cousin five years later. He was married by then, and already hung on the line. With his wife he had gone down to Alicia's country cottage. A summer night, just dark and very warm. After many exhortations she had brought into the little drawing-room her last finished picture. He could see her now placing it where the light fell, her tall, slight form already rather sharp and meagre, as the figures of some women grow at thirty, if they are not married; the nervous, fluttering look on her charming face, as though she could hardly bear this inspection; the way she raised her shoulder just a little as if to ward off an expected blow of condemnation. No need! It had been a beautiful thing, a quite surprisingly beautiful study of night. He remembered with what a really jealous ache he had gazed at it—a better thing than he had ever done himself. And, frankly, he had said so. Her eyes had shone with pleasure.

'Do you really like it? I tried so hard!'

'The day you show that, my dear,' he had said, 'your name's made!' She had clasped her hands and simply sighed: 'Oh, Dick!' He had felt quite happy in her happiness, and presently the three of them had taken their chairs out, beyond the curtains, on to the dark veranda, had talked a little, then somehow fallen silent. A wonderful warm, black, grape-bloom night, exquisitely gracious and inviting; the stars very high and white, the flowers glimmering in the garden-beds, and against the deep, dark blue, roses hanging, unearthly, stained with beauty. There was a scent of honeysuckle, he remembered, and many moths came fluttering by towards the tall, narrow chink of light between the curtains. Alicia had sat leaning forward, elbows on knees, ears buried in her hands. Probably they were silent because she sat like that. Once he heard her whisper to herself: 'Lovely, lovely! Oh, God! How lovely!' His wife, feeling the dew, had gone in, and he had followed; Alicia had not seemed to notice. But when she too came in, her eyes were glistening with tears. She said something about bed in a queer voice; they had taken candles and gone up. Next morning, going to her little studio to give her advice about that picture, he had been literally horrified to see it streaked with lines of white—Alicia, standing before it, was dashing her brush in broad smears across and across. She heard him and turned round. There was a hard red spot in either cheek, and she said in a quivering voice: 'It was blasphemy. That's all!' And turning her back on him she had gone on smearing it with white. Without a word, he had turned tail in simple disgust. Indeed, so deep had been his vexation at that wanton destruction of the best thing she had ever done or was ever likely to do, that he had avoided her for years. He had always had a horror of eccentricity. To have planted her foot firmly on the ladder of fame and then deliberately kicked it away; to have wantonly foregone this chance of making money—for she had but a mere pittance! It had seemed to him really too exasperating, a thing only to be explained by tapping one's forehead. Every now and then he still heard of her, living down there, spending her days out in the woods and fields, and sometimes even her nights, they said, and steadily growing poorer and thinner and more eccentric; becoming, in short, impossibly difficult, as only Englishwomen can. People would speak of her as 'such a dear', and talk of her charm, but always with that shrug which is hard to bear when applied to one's relations. What she did with the productions of her brush he never inquired, too disillusioned by that experience. Poor Alicia!

The pink berries glowed on the grey stone, and he had yet another memory. A family occasion when Uncle Martin Scudamore departed this life, and they all went up to bury him and hear his will. The old chap, whom they had looked on as a bit of a disgrace, money-grubbing up in the little grey Yorkshire town which owed its rise to his factory, was expected to make amends by his death, for he had never married—too sunk in industry, apparently, to have the time. By tacit agreement, his nephews and nieces had selected the Inn at Bolton Abbey, nearest beauty spot, for their stay. They had driven six miles to the funeral, in three carriages. Alicia had gone with him and his brother, the solicitor. In her plain black clothes she looked quite charming, in spite of the silver threads already thick in her fine dark hair, loosened by the moor wind. She had talked of painting to him with all her old enthusiasm, and her eyes had seemed to linger on his face as if she still had a little weakness for him. He had quite enjoyed that drive. They had come rather abruptly on the small grimy town clinging to the river banks, with old Martin's long, yellow-brick house dominating it, about two hundred yards above the mills. Suddenly, under the rug, he felt Alicia's hand seize his with a sort of desperation, for all the world as if she were clinging to something to support her. Indeed, he was sure she did not know it was his hand she squeezed. The cobbled streets, the muddy-looking water, the dingy, staring factories, the yellow, staring house, the little dark-clothed, dreadfully plain workpeople, all turned out to do a last honour to their creator; the hideous new grey church, the dismal service, the brand-new tombstones—and all of a glorious autumn day! It was inexpressibly sordid—too ugly for words! Afterwards the will was read to them seated decorously on bright mahogany chairs in the yellow mansion, a very satisfactory will, distributing in perfectly adjusted portions, to his own kinsfolk and nobody else, a very considerable wealth. Scudamore had listened to it dreamily, with his eyes fixed on an oily picture, thinking, 'My God! What a thing!' and longing to be back in the carriage smoking a cigar to take the reek of black clothes and sherry—sherry!—out of his nostrils. He happened to look at Alicia. Her eyes were closed;

her lips, always sweet-looking, quivered amusedly. And at that very moment the will came to her name. He saw those eyes open wide, and marked a beautiful pink flush, quite like that of old days, come into her thin cheeks. 'Splendid!' he had thought; 'it's really jolly for her. I *am* glad! Now she won't have to pinch. Splendid!' He shared with her to the full the surprised relief showing in her still beautiful face.

All the way home in the carriage he felt at least as happy over her good fortune as over his own, which had been substantial. He took her hand under the rug and squeezed it, and she answered with a long, gentle pressure, quite unlike the clutch when they were driving in. That same evening he strolled out to where the river curved below the Abbey. The sun had not quite set, and its last smoky radiance slanted into the burnished autumn woods. Some white-faced Herefords were grazing in lush grass, the river rippled and gleamed all over golden scales. About that scene was the magic which has so often startled the hearts of painters, the wistful gold—the enchantment of a dream. For some minutes he had gazed with delight which had in it a sort of despair. A little crisp rustle ran along the bushes; the leaves fluttered, then hung quite still. And he heard a voice—Alicia's—speaking. 'The lovely, lovely world!' And moving forward a step, he saw her standing on the river bank, braced against the trunk of a birch tree, her head thrown back, and her arms stretched wide apart as though to clasp the lovely world she had apostrophized. To have gone up to her would have been like breaking up a lovers' interview, and he turned round instead and went away.

A week later he heard from his brother that Alicia had refused her legacy. 'I don't want it,' her letter had said simply; 'I couldn't bear to take it. Give it to those poor people who live in that awful place.' Really eccentricity could go no farther! They decided to go down and see her. Such mad neglect of her own good must not be permitted without some effort to prevent it. They found her very thin and charming; humble, but quite obstinate in her refusal. 'Oh! I couldn't really! I should be so unhappy. Those poor little stunted people who made it all for him! That little, awful town! I simply couldn't be reminded. Don't talk about it, please. I'm quite all right as I am.' They had threatened her with lurid pictures of the workhouse and a destitute old age. To no purpose; she would not take the money. She had been forty when she refused that aid from heaven—forty, and already past any hope of marriage. For though Scudamore had never known for certain that she had ever wished or hoped for marriage, he had his theory—that all her eccentricity came from wasted sexual instinct. This last folly had seemed to him monstrous enough to be pathetic, and he no longer avoided her. Indeed, he would often walk over to tea in her little hermitage. With Uncle Martin's money he had bought and restored the beautiful old house over the River Arun, and was now only five miles from Alicia's, across country. She, too, would come tramping over at all hours, floating in with wild flowers or ferns, which she would put into water the moment she arrived. She had ceased to wear hats, and had by now a very doubtful reputation for sanity about the country-side. This was the period when Watts was on every painter's tongue, and he seldom saw Alicia without a disputation concerning that famous symbolist. Personally, he had no use for Watts, resenting his faulty drawing and crude allegories, but Alicia always maintained with her extravagant fervour that he was great because he tried to paint the soul of things. She especially loved a painting called 'Iris'—a female symbol of the rainbow, which indeed, in its floating eccentricity, had a certain resemblance to herself. 'Of course he failed,' she would say; 'he tried for the impossible and went on trying all his life. Oh! I can't bear your rules and catchwords, Dick; what's the good of them! Beauty's too big, too deep!' Poor Alicia! She was sometimes very wearing.

He never knew quite how it came about that she went abroad with them to Dauphiné in the autumn of 1904—a rather disastrous business. Never again would he take any one travelling who did not know how to come in out of the cold. It was a painter's country, and he had hired a little *château* in front of the Glandaz mountain—himself, his wife, their eldest girl, and Alicia. The adaptation of his famous manner to that strange scenery, its browns and French greys and filmy blues, so preoccupied him that he had scant time for becoming intimate with these hills and valleys. From the little gravelled terrace in front of the annexe, out of which he had made a studio, there was an absorbing view over the pantiled old town of Die. It glistened below in the early or late sunlight, flat-roofed and of pinkish yellow, with the dim, blue River Drôme circling one side, and cut, dark cypress trees dotting the vineyarded slopes. And he painted it continually. What Alicia did with herself they none of them very much knew, except that she would come in and talk ecstatically of things and beasts and people she had seen. One favourite haunt of hers they did visit—a ruined monastery high up in the amphitheatre of the Glandaz mountain. They had their lunch up there, a very charming and remote spot, where the watercourses and ponds and chapel of the old monks were still visible, though converted by the farmer to his use. Alicia left them abruptly in the middle of their praises, and they had not seen her again till they found her at home when they got back. It was almost as if she had resented laudation of her favourite haunt. She had brought in with her a great bunch of golden berries, of which none of them knew the name; berries almost as beautiful as these spindleberries glowing on the stone of the wall. And a fourth memory of Alicia came.

Christmas Eve, a sparkling frost, and every tree round the little *château* rimed so that they shone in the starlight as though dowered with cherry blossom. Never were more stars in clear black sky above the whitened earth. Down in the little town a few faint points of yellow light twinkled in the mountain wind keen as a razor's edge. A fantastically lovely night—quite 'Japanese', but cruelly cold. Five minutes on the terrace had been enough for all of them except Alicia. She—unaccountable, crazy creature—would not come in. Twice he had gone out to her, with commands, entreaties, and extra wraps; the third time he could not find her. She had deliberately avoided his onslaught and slid off somewhere to keep this mad vigil by frozen starlight. When at last she did come in she reeled as if drunk. They tried to make her really drunk, to put warmth back into her. No good! In two days she was down with double pneumonia; it was two months before she was up again—a very shadow of herself. There had never been much health in her since then. She floated like a ghost through life, a crazy ghost, who would steal away, goodness knew where, and come in with a flush in her withered cheeks, and her grey hair wild blown, carrying her spoil—some flower, some leaf, some tiny bird, or little soft rabbit. She never painted now, never even talked of it. They had made her give up her cottage and come to live with them, literally afraid that she would starve herself to death in her forgetfulness of everything. These spindleberries even! Why, probably, she had been right up this morning to that sunny chalk-pit in the lew of the Downs to get them, seven miles there and back, when you wouldn't think she could walk seven hundred yards, and as likely as not had lain there on the dewy grass looking up at the sky, as he had come on her sometimes. Poor Alicia! And once he had been within an ace of marrying her! A life spoiled! By what, if not by love of beauty? But who would have ever thought that the intangible could wreck a woman, deprive her of love, marriage, motherhood, of fame, of wealth, of health? And yet—by George!—it had!

Scudamore flipped the four pink berries off the wall. The radiance and the meandering milky waters; that swan against the brown tufted rushes; those far, filmy Downs—there was beauty! *Beauty!* But, damn it all—moderation! Moderation! And, turning his back on that prospect, which he had painted so many times in his celebrated manner, he went in, and up the expensively restored staircase to his studio. It had great windows on three sides, and perfect means for regulating light. Unfinished studies melted into walls so subdued that they looked like atmosphere. There were no completed pictures—they sold too fast. As he walked over to his easel his eye was caught by a spray of colour—the branch of spindleberries set in water, ready for him to use, just where the pale sunlight fell so that their delicate colour might glow and the few tiny drops of moisture still clinging to them shine. For a second he saw Alicia herself as she must have looked, setting them there, her transparent hands hovering, her eyes shining, that grey hair of hers all fine and loose. The vision vanished! But what had made her bring them after that horrified 'God!' when he spoke of using them? Was it her way of saying: 'Forgive me for being rude'? Really she was pathetic, that poor devotee! The spindleberries glowed in their silver-lustre jug, sprayed up against the sunlight. They looked triumphant—as well they might, who stood for that which had ruined—or was it saved?—a life! Alicia! She had made a pretty mess of it, and yet who knew what secret raptures she had felt with her subtle lover, Beauty, by starlight and sunlight and moonlight, in the fields and woods, on the hilltops, and by riverside? Flowers, and the flight of birds, and the ripple of the wind, and all the shifting play of light and colour which made a man despair when he wanted to use them; she had taken them, hugged them to her with no afterthought, and been happy! Who could say that she had missed the prize of life? Who could say it? . . . Spindleberries! A bunch of spindleberries to set such doubts astir in him! Why, what was beauty but just the extra value which certain forms and colours, blended, gave to things—just the extra value in the human market! Nothing else on earth, nothing! And the spindleberries glowed against the sunlight, delicate, remote!

Taking his palette, he mixed crimson lake, white, and ultramarine. What was that? Who sighed, away out there behind him? Nothing!

'Damn it all!' he thought; 'this is childish. This is as bad as Alicia!' And he set to work to paint in his celebrated manner—spindleberries.

RICHARD HUGHES

A Night at a Cottage

On the evening that I am considering I passed by some ten or twenty cosy barns and sheds without finding one to my liking: for Worcestershire lanes are devious and muddy, and it was nearly dark when I found an empty cottage set back from the road in a little bedraggled garden. There had been heavy rain earlier in the day, and the straggling fruit-trees still wept over it.

But the roof looked sound, there seemed no reason why it should not be fairly dry inside—as dry, at any rate, as I was likely to find anywhere.

I decided: and with a long look up the road, and a long look down the road, I drew an iron bar from the lining of my coat and forced the door, which was only held by a padlock and two staples. Inside, the darkness was damp and heavy: I struck a match, and with its haloed light I saw the black mouth of a passage somewhere ahead of me: and then it spluttered out. So I closed the door carefully, though I had little reason to fear passers-by at such a dismal hour in so remote a lane: and lighting another match, I crept down this passage to a little room at the far end, where the air was a bit clearer, for all that the window was boarded across. Moreover, there was a little rusted stove in this room: and thinking it too dark for any to see the smoke, I ripped up part of the wainscot with my knife, and soon was boiling my tea over a bright, small fire, and drying some of the day's rain out of my steamy clothes. Presently I piled the stove with wood to its top bar, and setting my boots where they would best dry, I stretched my body out to sleep.

I cannot have slept very long, for when I woke the fire was still burning brightly. It is not easy to sleep for long together on the level boards of a floor, for the limbs grow numb, and any movement wakes. I turned over, and was about to go again to sleep when I was startled to hear steps in the passage. As I have said, the window was boarded, and there was no other door from the little room—no cupboard even—in which to hide. It occurred to me rather grimly that there was nothing to do but to sit up and face the music, and that would probably mean being haled back to Worcester jail, which I had left two bare days before, and where, for various reasons, I had no anxiety to be seen again.

The stranger did not hurry himself, but presently walked slowly down the passage, attracted by the light of the fire: and when he came in he did not seem to notice me where I lay huddled in a corner, but walked straight over to the stove and warmed his hands at it. He was dripping wet; wetter than I should have thought it possible for a man to get, even on such a rainy night: and his clothes were old and worn. The water dripped from him on to the floor: he wore no hat, and the straight hair over his eyes dripped water that sizzled spitefully on the embers.

It occurred to me at once that he was no lawful citizen, but another wanderer like myself; a gentleman of the Road; so I gave him some sort of greeting, and we were presently in conversation. He complained much of the cold and the wet, and huddled himself over the fire, his teeth chattering and his face an ill white.

'No,' I said, 'it is no decent weather for the Road,

this. But I wonder this cottage isn't more frequented, for it's a tidy little bit of a cottage.'

Outside the pale dead sunflowers and giant weeds stirred in the rain.

'Time was,' he answered, 'there wasn't a tighter little cot in the co-anty, nor a purtier garden. A regular little parlour, she was. But now no folk'll live in it, and there's very few tramps will stop here either.'

There were none of the rags and tins and broken food about that you find in a place where many beggars are used to stay.

'Why 's that?' I asked.

He gave a very troubled sigh before answering.

'Gho-asts,' he said; 'gho-asts. Him that lived here. It is a mighty sad tale, and I'll not tell it you: but the upshot of it was that he drowned himself, down to the mill-pond. All slimy, he was, and floating, when they pulled him out of it. There are fo-aks have seen un floating on the pond, and fo-aks have seen un set round the corner of the school, waiting for his childer. Seems as if he had forgotten, like, how they were all gone dead, and the why he drowned hisself. But there are some say he walks up and down this cottage, up and down; like when the small-pox had 'em, and they couldn't sleep but if they heard his feet going up and down by their do-ars. Drownded hisself down to the pond, he did: and now he Walks.'

The stranger sighed again, and I could hear the water squelch in his boots as he moved himself.

'But it doesn't do for the like of us to get superstitious,' I answered. 'It wouldn't do for us to get seeing ghosts, or many 's the wet night we'd be lying in the roadway.'

'No,' he said; 'no, it wouldn't do at all. I never had belief in Walks myself.'

I laughed.

'Nor I that,' I said. 'I never see ghosts, whoever may.'

He looked at me again in his queer melancholy fashion.

'No,' he said. ''Spect you don't ever. Some folk do-an't. It's hard enough for poor fellows to have no money to their lodging, apart from gho-asts sceering them.'

'It's the coppers, not spooks, make me sleep uneasy,' said I. 'What with coppers, and meddlesome-minded folk, it isn't easy to get a night's rest nowadays.'

The water was still oozing from his clothes all about the floor, and a dank smell went up from him.

'God! man,' I cried, 'can't you *never* get dry?'

'Dry?' He made a little coughing laughter. 'Dry? I shan't never be dry . . . 'tisn't the likes of us that ever get dry, be it wet *or* fine, winter *or* summer. See that!'

He thrust his muddy hands up to the wrist in the fire, glowering over it fiercely and madly. But I caught up my two boots and ran crying out into the night.

MONTAGUE JAMES

Casting the Runes

April 15*th*, 190–.

DEAR SIR,—I am requested by the Council of the —— Association to return to you the draft of a paper on *The Truth of Alchemy*, which you have been good enough to offer to read at our forthcoming meeting, and to inform you that the Council do not see their way to including it in the programme.

I am,

Yours faithfully,

—— *Secretary*.

April 18*th*.

DEAR SIR,—I am sorry to say that my engagements do not permit of my affording you an interview on the subject of your proposed paper. Nor do our laws allow of your discussing the matter with a Committee of our Council, as you suggest. Please allow me to assure you that the fullest consideration was given to the draft which you submitted, and that it was not declined without having been referred to the judgement of a most competent authority. No personal question (it can hardly be necessary for me to add) can have had the slightest influence on the decision of the Council.

Believe me (*ut supra*).

April 20*th*.

The Secretary of the —— Association begs respectfully to inform Mr. Karswell that it is impossible for him to communicate the name of any person or persons to whom the draft of Mr. Karswell's paper may have been submitted; and further desires to intimate that he cannot undertake to reply to any further letters on this subject.

'And who *is* Mr. Karswell?' inquired the Secretary's wife. She had called at his office, and (perhaps unwarrantably) had picked up the last of these three letters, which the typist had just brought in.

'Why, my dear, just at present Mr. Karswell is a very angry man. But I don't know much about him otherwise, except that he is a person of wealth, his address is Lufford Abbey, Warwickshire, and he's an alchemist, apparently, and wants to tell us all about it; and that's about all—except that I don't want to meet him for the next week or two. Now, if you're ready to leave this place, I am.'

'What have you been doing to make him angry?' asked Mrs. Secretary.

'The usual thing, my dear, the usual thing: he sent in a draft of a paper he wanted to read at the next meeting, and we referred it to Edward Dunning—almost the only man in England who knows about these things—and he said it was perfectly hopeless, so we declined it. So Karswell has been pelting me with letters ever since. The last thing he wanted was the name of the man we referred his nonsense to; you saw my answer to that. But don't you say anything about it, for goodness' sake.'

'I should think not, indeed. Did I ever do such a thing? I do hope, though, he won't get to know that it was poor Mr. Dunning.'

'Poor Mr. Dunning? I don't know why you call him that; he's a very happy man, is Dunning. Lots of hobbies and a comfortable home, and all his time to himself.'

'I only meant I should be sorry for him if this man got hold of his name, and came and bothered him.'

'Oh, ah! yes. I dare say he would be poor Mr. Dunning then.'

The Secretary and his wife were lunching out, and the friends to whose house they were bound were Warwickshire people. So Mrs. Secretary had already settled it in her own mind that she would question them judiciously about Mr. Karswell. But she was saved the trouble of leading up to the subject, for the hostess said to the host, before many minutes had passed, 'I saw the Abbot of Lufford this morning.' The host whistled. '*Did* you? What in the world brings him up to town?' 'Goodness knows; he was coming out of the British Museum gate as I drove past.' It was not unnatural that Mrs. Secretary should inquire whether this was a real Abbot who was being spoken of. 'Oh no, my dear: only a neighbour of ours in the country who bought Lufford Abbey a few years ago. His real name is Karswell.' 'Is he a friend of yours?' asked Mr. Secretary, with a private wink to his wife. The question let loose a torrent of declamation. There was really nothing to be said for Mr. Karswell. Nobody knew what he did with himself: his servants were a horrible set of people; he had invented a new religion for himself, and practised no one could tell what appalling rites; he was very easily offended, and never forgave anybody; he had a dreadful face (so the lady insisted, her husband somewhat demurring); he never did a kind action, and whatever influence he did exert was mischievous. 'Do the poor man justice, dear,' the husband interrupted. 'You forget the treat he gave the school children.' 'Forget it, indeed! But I'm glad you mentioned it, because it gives an idea of the man. Now, Florence, listen to this. The first winter he was at Lufford this delightful neighbour of ours wrote to the clergyman of his parish (he's not ours, but we know him very well) and offered to show the school children some magic-lantern slides. He said he had some new kinds, which he thought would interest them. Well, the clergyman was rather surprised, because Mr. Karswell had shown himself inclined to be unpleasant to the children—complaining of their trespassing, or something of the sort; but of course he accepted, and the evening was fixed, and our friend went himself to see that everything went right. He said he never had been so thankful for anything as that his own children were all prevented from being there: they were at a children's party at our house, as a matter of fact. Because this Mr. Karswell had evidently set out with the intention of frightening these poor village children out of their wits, and I do believe, if he had been allowed to go on, he would actually have done so. He began with some comparatively mild things. Red Riding Hood was one, and even then, Mr. Farrer said, the wolf was so dreadful that several of the smaller children had to be taken out: and he said Mr. Karswell began the story by producing a noise like a wolf howling in the distance, which was the most gruesome thing he had ever heard. All the slides he showed, Mr. Farrer said, were most clever; they were absolutely realistic, and where he had got them or how he worked them he could not imagine. Well, the show went on, and the stories kept on becoming a little more terrifying each time, and the children were mesmerized into complete silence. At last he produced a series which represented a little boy passing through his own park—Lufford, I mean—in the evening. Every child in the room could recognize the place from the pictures. And this poor boy was followed, and at last pursued and overtaken, and either torn in pieces or somehow made away with, by a horrible hopping creature in white, which you saw first dodging about among the trees, and gradually it appeared more and more plainly. Mr. Farrer said it gave him one of the worst nightmares he ever remembered, and what it must have meant to the children doesn't bear thinking of. Of course this was too much, and he spoke very sharply indeed to Mr. Karswell, and said it couldn't go on. All *he* said was: "Oh, you think it's time to bring our little show to an end and send them home to their beds? *Very* well!" And then, if you please, he switched on another slide, which showed a great mass of snakes, centipedes, and disgusting creatures with wings, and somehow or other he made it seem as if they were climbing out of the picture and getting in amongst the audience; and this was accompanied by a sort of dry rustling noise which sent the children nearly mad, and of course they stampeded. A good many of them were rather hurt in getting out of the room, and I don't suppose one of them closed an eye that night. There was the most dreadful trouble in the village afterwards. Of course the mothers threw a good part of the blame on poor Mr. Farrer, and, if they could have got past the gates, I believe the fathers would have broken every window in the Abbey. Well, now, that's Mr. Karswell: that's the Abbot of Lufford, my dear, and you can imagine how we covet *his* society.'

'Yes, I think he has all the possibilities of a distinguished criminal, has Karswell,' said the host. 'I should be sorry for any one who got into his bad books.'

'Is he the man, or am I mixing him up with some one else?' asked the Secretary (who for some minutes had been wearing the frown of the man who is trying to recollect something). 'Is he the man who brought out a *History of Witchcraft* some time back—ten years or more?'

'That's the man; do you remember the reviews of it?'

'Certainly I do; and what's equally to the point, I knew the author of the most incisive of the lot. So did you: you must remember John Harrington; he was at John's in our time.'

'Oh, very well indeed, though I don't think I saw or heard anything of him between the time I went down and the day I read the account of the inquest on him.'

'Inquest?' said one of the ladies. 'What has happened to him?'

'Why, what happened was that he fell out of a tree and broke his neck. But the puzzle was, what could have induced him to get up there. It was a mysterious business, I must say. Here was this man—not an athletic fellow, was he? and with no eccentric twist about him that was ever noticed—walking home along a country road late in the evening—no tramps about—well known and liked in the place—and he suddenly begins to run like mad, loses his hat and stick, and finally shins up a tree—quite a difficult tree—growing in the hedgerow: a dead branch gives way, and he comes down with it and breaks his neck, and there he's found next morning with the most dreadful face of fear on him that could be imagined. It was pretty evident, of course, that he had been chased by something, and people talked of savage dogs, and beasts escaped out of menageries; but there was nothing to be made of that. That was in '89, and I believe his brother Henry (whom I remember as well at Cambridge, but *you* probably don't) has been trying to get on the track of an explanation ever since. He, of course, insists there was malice in it, but I don't know. It's difficult to see how it could have come in.'

After a time the talk reverted to the *History of Witchcraft*. 'Did you ever look into it?' asked the host.

'Yes, I did,' said the Secretary. 'I went so far as to read it.'

'Was it as bad as it was made out to be?'

'Oh, in point of style and form, quite hopeless. It deserved all the pulverizing it got. But, besides that, it was an evil book. The man believed every word of what he was saying, and I'm very much mistaken if he hadn't tried the greater part of his receipts.'

'Well, I only remember Harrington's review of it, and I must say if I'd been the author it would have quenched my literary ambition for good. I should never have held up my head again.'

'It hasn't had that effect in the present case. But come, it's half-past three; I must be off.'

On the way home the Secretary's wife said, 'I do hope that horrible man won't find out that Mr. Dunning had anything to do with the rejection of his paper.' 'I don't think there's much chance of that,' said the Secretary. 'Dunning won't mention it himself, for these matters are confidential, and none of us will for the same reason. Karswell won't know his name, for Dunning hasn't published anything on the same subject yet. The only danger is that Karswell might find out, if he was to ask the British Museum people who was in the habit of consulting alchemical manuscripts: I can't very well tell them not to mention Dunning, can I? It would set them talking at once. Let's hope it won't occur to him.'

However, Mr. Karswell was an astute man.

This much is in the way of prologue. On an evening rather later in the same week, Mr. Edward Dunning was returning from the British Museum, where he had been engaged in Research, to the comfortable house in a suburb where he lived alone, tended by two excellent women who had been long with him. There is nothing to be added by way of description of him to what we have heard already. Let us follow him as he takes his sober course homewards.

A train took him to within a mile or two of his house, and an electric tram a stage farther. The line ended at a point some three hundred yards from his front door. He had had enough of reading when he got into the car, and indeed the light was not such as to allow him to do more than study the advertisements on the panes of glass that faced him as he sat. As was not unnatural, the advertisements in this particular line of cars were objects of his frequent contemplation, and, with the possible exception of the brilliant and convincing dialogue between Mr. Lamplough and an eminent K.C. on the subject of Pyretic Saline, none of them afforded much scope to his imagination. I am wrong: there was one at the corner of the car farthest from him which did not seem familiar. It was in blue letters on a yellow ground, and all that he could read of it was a name—John Harrington—and something like a date. It could be of no interest to him to know more; but for all that, as the car emptied, he was just curious enough to move along the seat until he could read it well. He felt to a slight extent repaid for his trouble; the advertisement was *not* of the usual type. It ran thus: 'In memory of John Harrington, F.S.A., of The Laurels, Ashbrooke. Died Sept. 18th, 1889. Three months were allowed.'

The car stopped. Mr. Dunning, still contemplating the blue letters on the yellow ground, had to be stimulated to rise by a word from the conductor. 'I beg your pardon,' he said, 'I was looking at that advertisement; it's a very odd one, isn't it?' The conductor read it slowly. 'Well, my word,' he said, 'I never see that one before. Well, that is a cure, ain't it? Some one bin up to their jokes 'ere, I should think.' He got out a duster and applied it, not without saliva, to the pane and then to the outside. 'No,' he said, returning, 'that ain't no transfer; seems to me as if it was reg'lar *in* the glass, what I mean in the substance, as you may say. Don't you think so, sir?' Mr. Dunning examined it and rubbed it with his glove, and agreed. 'Who looks after these advertisements, and gives leave for them to be put up? I wish you would inquire. I will just take a note of the words.' At this moment there came a call from the driver: 'Look alive, George, time's up.' 'All right, all right; there's somethink else what's up at this end. You come and look at this 'ere glass.' 'What's gorn with the glass?' said the driver, approaching. 'Well, and oo's 'Arrington? What's it all about?' 'I was just asking who was responsible for putting the advertisements up in your cars, and saying it would be as well to make some inquiry about this one.' 'Well, sir, that's all done at the Company's office, that work is: it's our Mr. Timms, I believe, looks into that. When we put up to-night I'll leave word, and per'aps I'll be able to tell you to-morrer if you 'appen to be coming this way.'

This was all that passed that evening. Mr. Dunning did just go to the trouble of looking up Ashbrooke, and found that it was in Warwickshire.

Next day he went to town again. The car (it was the same car) was too full in the morning to allow of his getting a word with the conductor: he could only be sure that the curious advertisement had been made away with. The close of the day brought a further element of mystery into the transaction. He had missed the tram, or else preferred walking home, but at a rather late hour, while he was at work in his study, one of the maids came to say that two men from the tramways were very anxious to speak to him. This was a reminder of the advertisement, which he had, he says, nearly forgotten. He had the men in—they were the conductor and driver of the car—and when the matter of refreshment had been attended to, asked what Mr. Timms had had to say about the advertisement. 'Well, sir, that's what we took the liberty to step round about,' said the conductor. 'Mr. Timms 'e give William 'ere the rough side of his tongue about that: 'cordin' to 'im there warn't no advertisement of that description sent in, nor ordered, nor paid for, nor put up, nor nothink, let alone not bein' there, and we was playing the fool takin' up his time. "Well," I says, "if that's the case, all I ask of you, Mr. Timms," I says, "is to take and look at it for yourself," I says. "Of course if it ain't there," I says, "you may take and call me what you like." "Right," he says, "I will": and we went straight off. Now, I leave it to you, sir, if that ad., as we term 'em, with 'Arrington on it warn't as plain as ever you see anythink—blue letters on yeller glass, and as I says at the time, and you borne me out, reg'lar *in* the glass, because, if you remember, you recollect of me swabbing it with my duster.' 'To be sure I do, quite clearly—well?' 'You may say well, I don't think. Mr. Timms he gets in that car with a light—no, he telled William to 'old the light outside. "Now," he says, "where's your precious ad. what we've 'eard so much about?" " 'Ere it is," I says, "Mr. Timms," and I laid my 'and on it.' The conductor paused.

'Well,' said Mr. Dunning, 'it was gone, I suppose. Broken?'

'Broke!—not it. There warn't, if you'll believe me, no more trace of them letters—blue letters they was—on that piece o' glass, than—well, it's no good *me* talkin'. *I* never see such a thing. I leave it to William here if—but there, as I says, where's the benefit in me going on about it?'

'And what did Mr. Timms say?'

'Why 'e did what I give 'im leave to—called us pretty much anythink he liked, and I don't know as I blame him so much neither. But what we thought, William and me did, was as we seen you take down a bit of a note about that—well, that letterin'——'

'I certainly did that, and I have it now. Did you wish me to speak to Mr. Timms myself, and show it to him? Was that what you came in about?'

'There, didn't I say as much?' said William. 'Deal with a gent if you can get on the track of one, that's my word. Now perhaps, George, you'll allow as I ain't took you very far wrong to-night.'

'Very well, William, very well; no need for you to go on as if you'd 'ad to frog's-march me 'ere. I come quiet, didn't I? All the same for that, we 'adn't ought to take up your time this way, sir; but if it so 'appened you could find time to step round to the Company's orfice in the morning and tell Mr. Timms what you seen for yourself, we should lay under a very 'igh obligation to you for the trouble. You see it ain't bein' called—well, one thing and another, as we mind, but if they got it into their 'ead at the orfice as we seen things as warn't there, why, one thing leads to another, and where we should be a twelvemunce 'ence—well, you can understand what I mean.'

Amid further elucidations of the proposition, George, conducted by William, left the room.

The incredulity of Mr. Timms (who had a nodding acquaintance with Mr. Dunning) was greatly modified on the following day by what the latter could tell and show him; and any bad mark that might have been attached to the names of William and George was not suffered to remain on the Company's books; but explanation there was none.

Mr. Dunning's interest in the matter was kept alive by an incident of the following afternoon. He was walking from his club to the train, and he noticed some way ahead a man with a handful of leaflets such as are distributed to passers-by by agents of enterprising firms. This agent had not chosen a very crowded street for his operations: in fact, Mr. Dunning did not see him get rid of a single leaflet before he himself reached the spot. One was thrust into his hand as he passed: the hand that gave it touched his, and he experienced a sort of little shock as it did so. It seemed unnaturally rough and hot. He looked in passing at the giver, but the impression he got was so unclear that, however much he tried to reckon it up subsequently, nothing would come. He was walking quickly, and as he went on glanced at the paper. It was a blue one. The name of Harrington in large capitals caught his eye. He stopped, startled, and felt for his glasses. The next instant the leaflet was twitched out of his hand by a man who hurried past, and was irrecoverably gone. He ran back a few paces, but where was the passer-by? and where the distributor?

It was in a somewhat pensive frame of mind that Mr. Dunning passed on the following day into the Select Manuscript Room of the British Museum, and filled up tickets for Harley 3586, and some other volumes. After a few minutes they were brought to him, and he was settling the one he wanted first upon the desk, when he thought he heard his own name whispered behind him. He turned round hastily, and in doing so, brushed his little portfolio of loose papers on to the floor. He saw no one he recognized except one of the staff in charge of the room, who nodded to him, and he proceeded to pick up his papers. He thought he had them all, and was turning to begin work, when a stout gentleman at the table behind him, who was just rising to leave, and had collected his own belongings, touched him on the shoulder, saying, 'May I give you this? I think it should be yours,' and handed him a missing quire. 'It is mine, thank you,' said Mr. Dunning. In another moment the man had left the room. Upon finishing his work for the afternoon, Mr. Dunning had some conversation with the assistant in charge, and took occasion to ask who the stout gentleman was. 'Oh, he's a man named Karswell,' said the assistant; 'he was asking me a week ago who were the great authorities on alchemy, and of course I told him you were the only one in the country. I'll see if I can't catch him: he'd like to meet you, I'm sure.'

'For heaven's sake don't dream of it!' said Mr. Dunning, 'I'm particularly anxious to avoid him.'

'Oh! very well,' said the assistant, 'he doesn't come here often: I dare say you won't meet him.'

More than once on the way home that day Mr. Dunning confessed to himself that he did not look forward with his usual cheerfulness to a solitary evening. It seemed to him that something ill defined and impalpable had stepped in between him and his fellow men—had taken him in charge, as it were. He wanted to sit close up to his neighbours in the train and in the tram, but as luck would have it both train and car were markedly empty. The conductor George was thoughtful, and appeared to be absorbed in calculations as to the number of passengers. On arriving at his house he found Dr. Watson, his medical man, on his doorstep. 'I've had to upset your household arrangements, I'm sorry to say, Dunning. Both your servants *hors de combat*. In fact, I've had to send them to the Nursing Home.'

'Good heavens! what's the matter?'

'It's something like ptomaine poisoning, I should think: you've not suffered yourself, I can see, or you wouldn't be walking about. I think they'll pull through all right.'

'Dear, dear! Have you any idea what brought it on?'

'Well, they tell me they bought some shell-fish from a hawker at their dinner-time. It's odd. I've made inquiries, but I can't find that any hawker has been to other houses in the street. I couldn't send word to you; they won't be back for a bit yet. You come and dine with me to-night, anyhow, and we can make arrangements for going on. Eight o'clock. Don't be too anxious.'

The solitary evening was thus obviated; at the expense

of some distress and inconvenience, it is true. Mr. Dunning spent the time pleasantly enough with the doctor (a rather recent settler), and returned to his lonely home at about 11.30. The night he passed is not one on which he looks back with any satisfaction. He was in bed and the light was out. He was wondering if the charwoman would come early enough to get him hot water next morning, when he heard the unmistakable sound of his study door opening. No step followed it on the passage floor, but the sound must mean mischief, for he knew that he had shut the door that evening after putting his papers away in his desk. It was rather shame than courage that induced him to slip out into the passage and lean over the banister in his nightgown, listening. No light was visible; no further sound came: only a gust of warm, or even hot air played for an instant round his shins. He went back and decided to lock himself into his room. There was more unpleasantness, however. Either an economical suburban company had decided that their light would not be required in the small hours, and had stopped working, or else something was wrong with the meter; the effect was in any case that the electric light was off. The obvious course was to find a match, and also to consult his watch: he might as well know how many hours of discomfort awaited him. So he put his hand into the well-known nook under the pillow: only, it did not get so far. What he touched was, according to his account, a mouth, with teeth, and with hair about it, and, he declares, not the mouth of a human being. I do not think it is any use to guess what he said or did; but he was in a spare room with the door locked and his ear to it before he was clearly conscious again. And there he spent the rest of a most miserable night, looking every moment for some fumbling at the door: but nothing came.

The venturing back to his own room in the morning was attended with many listenings and quiverings. The door stood open, fortunately, and the blinds were up (the servants had been out of the house before the hour of drawing them down); there was, to be short, no trace of an inhabitant. The watch, too, was in its usual place; nothing was disturbed, only the wardrobe door had swung open, in accordance with its confirmed habit. A ring at the back door now announced the charwoman, who had been ordered the night before, and nerved Mr. Dunning, after letting her in, to continue his search in other parts of the house. It was equally fruitless.

The day thus begun went on dismally enough. He dared not go to the Museum: in spite of what the assistant had said, Karswell might turn up there, and Dunning felt he could not cope with a probably hostile stranger. His own house was odious; he hated sponging on the doctor. He spent some little time in a call at the Nursing Home, where he was slightly cheered by a good report of his housekeeper and maid. Towards lunch-time he betook himself to his club, again experiencing a gleam of satisfaction at seeing the Secretary of the Association. At luncheon Dunning told his friend the more material of his woes, but could not bring himself to speak of those that weighed most heavily on his spirits. 'My poor dear man,' said the Secretary, 'what an upset! Look here: we're alone at home, absolutely. You must put up with us. Yes! no excuse: send your things in this afternoon.' Dunning was unable to stand out: he was, in truth, becoming acutely anxious, as the hours went on, as to what that night might have waiting for him. He was almost happy as he hurried home to pack up.

His friends, when they had time to take stock of him, were rather shocked at his lorn appearance, and did their best to keep him up to the mark. Not altogether without success: but, when the two men were smoking alone later, Dunning became dull again. Suddenly he said, 'Gayton, I believe that alchemist man knows it was I who got his paper rejected.' Gayton whistled. 'What makes you think that?' he said. Dunning told of his conversation with the Museum assistant, and Gayton could only agree that the guess seemed likely to be correct. 'Not that I care much,' Dunning went on, 'only it might be a nuisance if we were to meet. He's a bad-tempered party, I imagine.' Conversation dropped again; Gayton became more and more strongly impressed with the desolateness that came over Dunning's face and bearing, and finally—though with a considerable effort—he asked him point-blank whether something serious was not bothering him. Dunning gave an exclamation of relief. 'I was perishing to get it off my mind,' he said. 'Do you know anything about a man named John Harrington?' Gayton was thoroughly startled, and at the moment could only ask why. Then the complete story of Dunning's experiences came out—what had happened in the tramcar, in his own house, and in the street, the troubling of spirit that had crept over him, and still held him; and he ended with the question he had begun with. Gayton was at a loss how to answer him. To tell the story of Harrington's end would perhaps be right; only, Dunning was in a nervous state, the story was a grim one, and he could not help asking himself whether there were not a connecting link between these two cases, in the person of Karswell. It was a difficult concession for a scientific man, but it could be eased by the phrase 'hypnotic suggestion'. In the end he decided that his answer to-night should be guarded; he would talk the situation over with his wife. So he said that he had known Harrington at Cambridge, and believed he had died suddenly in 1889, adding a few details about the man and his published work. He did talk over the matter with Mrs. Gayton, and, as he had anticipated, she leapt at once to the conclusion which had been hovering before him. It was she who reminded him of the surviving brother, Henry Harrington, and she also who suggested that he might be got hold of by means of their hosts of the day before. 'He might be a hopeless crank,' objected Gayton. 'That could be ascertained from the Bennetts, who knew him,' Mrs. Gayton retorted; and she undertook to see the Bennetts the very next day.

It is not necessary to tell in further detail the steps by which Henry Harrington and Dunning were brought together.

The next scene that does require to be narrated is a conversation that took place between the two. Dunning had told Harrington of the strange ways in which the dead man's name had been brought before him, and had said something, besides, of his own subsequent experiences. Then he had asked if Harrington was disposed, in return, to recall any of the circumstances connected with his brother's death. Harrington's surprise at what he heard can be imagined: but his reply was readily given.

'John,' he said, 'was in a very odd state, undeniably, from time to time, during some weeks before, though not immediately before, the catastrophe. There were several things; the principal notion he had was that he thought he was being followed. No doubt he was an impressionable man, but he never had had such fancies as this before. I cannot get it out of my mind that there was ill-will at work, and what you tell me about yourself reminds me very much of my brother. Can you think of any possible connecting link?'

'There is just one that has been taking shape vaguely in my mind. I've been told that your brother reviewed a book very severely not long before he died, and just lately I have happened to cross the path of the man who wrote that book in a way he would resent.'

'Don't tell me the man was called Karswell.'

'Why not? that is exactly his name.'

Henry Harrington leant back. 'That is final to my mind. Now I must explain further. From something he said, I feel sure that my brother John was beginning to believe—very much against his will—that Karswell was at the bottom of his trouble. I want to tell you what seems to me to have a bearing on the situation. My brother was a great musician, and used to run up to concerts in town. He came back, three months before he died, from one of these, and gave me his programme to look at—an analytical programme: he always kept them. "I nearly missed this one," he said. "I suppose I must have dropped it: anyhow, I was looking for it under my seat and in my pockets and so on, and my neighbour offered me his: said 'might he give it me, he had no further use for it,' and he went away just afterwards. I don't know who he was—a stout, clean-shaven man. I should have been sorry to miss it; of course I could have bought another, but this cost me nothing." At another time he told me that he had been very uncomfortable both on the way to his hotel and during the night. I piece things together now in thinking it over. Then, not very long after, he was going over these programmes, putting them in order to have them bound up, and in this particular one (which by the way I had hardly glanced at), he found quite near the beginning a strip of paper with some very odd writing on it in red and black—most carefully done—it looked to me more like Runic letters than anything else. "Why," he said, "this must belong to my fat neighbour. It looks as if it might be worth returning to him; it may be a copy of something; evidently some one has taken trouble over it. How can I find his address?" We talked it over for a little and agreed that it wasn't worth advertising about, and that my brother had better look out for the man at the next concert, to which he was going very soon. The paper was lying on the book and we were both by the fire; it was a cold, windy summer evening. I suppose the door blew open, though I didn't notice it: at any rate a gust—a warm gust it was—came quite suddenly between us, took the paper and blew it straight into the fire: it was light, thin paper, and flared and went up the chimney in a single ash. "Well," I said, "you can't give it back now." He said nothing for a minute: then rather crossly, "No, I can't; but why you should keep on saying so I don't know." I remarked that I didn't say it more than once. "Not more than four times, you mean," was all he said. I remember all that very clearly, without any good reason; and now to come to the point. I don't know if you looked at that book of Karswell's which my unfortunate brother reviewed. It's not likely that you should: but I did, both before his death and after it. The first time we made game of it together. It was written in no style at all—split infinitives, and every sort of thing that makes an Oxford gorge rise. Then there was nothing that the man didn't swallow: mixing up classical myths, and stories out of the *Golden Legend* with reports of savage customs of to-day—all very proper, no doubt, if you know how to use them, but he didn't: he seemed to put the *Golden Legend* and the *Golden Bough* exactly on a par, and to believe both: a pitiable exhibition, in short. Well, after the misfortune, I looked over the book again. It was no better than before, but the impression which it left this time on my mind was different. I suspected—as I told you—that Karswell had borne ill will to my brother, even that he was in some way responsible for what had happened; and now his book seemed to me to be a very sinister performance indeed. One chapter in particular struck me, in which he spoke of "casting the Runes" on people, either for the purpose of gaining their affection or of getting them out of the way—perhaps more especially the latter: he spoke of all this in a way that really seemed to me to imply actual knowledge. I've not time to go into details, but the upshot is that I am pretty sure from information received that the civil man at the concert was Karswell: I suspect—I more than suspect—that the paper was of importance: and I do believe that if my brother had been able to give it back, he might have been alive now. Therefore, it occurs to me to ask you whether you have anything to put beside what I have told you.'

By way of answer, Dunning had the episode in the Manuscript Room at the British Museum to relate.

'Then he did actually hand you some papers; have you examined them? No? because we must, if you'll allow it, look at them at once, and very carefully.'

They went to the still-empty house—empty, for the two servants were not yet able to return to work. Dunning's portfolio of papers was gathering dust on the writing-table. In it were the quires of small-sized scribbling paper which he used for his transcripts: and from one of these, as he took it up, there slipped and fluttered out into the room with uncanny quickness, a strip of thin light paper. The window was open, but Harrington slammed it to, just in time to intercept the paper, which he caught. 'I thought so,' he said; 'it might be the identical thing that was given to my brother. You'll have to look out, Dunning; this may mean something quite serious for you.'

A long consultation took place. The paper was narrowly examined. As Harrington had said, the characters on it were more like Runes than anything else, but not decipherable by either man, and both hesitated to copy them, for fear, as they confessed, of perpetuating whatever evil purpose they might conceal. So it has remained impossible (if I may anticipate a little) to ascertain what was conveyed in this curious message or commission. Both Dunning and Harrington are firmly convinced that it had the effect of bringing its possessors into very undesirable company. That it must be returned to the source whence it came they were agreed, and further, that the only safe and certain way was that of personal service; and here contrivance would be necessary, for Dunning was known by sight to Karswell. He must, for one thing, alter his appearance by shaving his beard. But then might not the blow fall first? Harrington thought they could time it. He knew the date of the concert at which the 'black spot' had been put on his brother: it was June 18th. The death had followed on September 18th. Dunning reminded him that three months had been mentioned on the inscription on the car-window. 'Perhaps,' he added, with a cheerless laugh, 'mine may be a bill at three months too. I believe I can fix it by my diary. Yes, April 23rd was the day at the Museum; that brings us to July 23rd. Now, you know, it becomes extremely important to me to know anything you will tell me about the progress of your brother's trouble, if it is possible for you to speak of it.'

'Of course. Well, the sense of being watched whenever he was alone was the most distressing thing to him. After a time I took to sleeping in his room, and he was the better for that: still, he talked a great deal in his sleep. What about? Is it wise to dwell on that, at least before things are straightened out? I think not, but I can tell you this: two things came for him by post during those weeks, both with a London postmark, and addressed in a commercial hand. One was a woodcut of Bewick's, roughly torn out of the page: one which shows a moonlit road and a man walking along it, followed by an awful demon creature. Under it were written the lines out of the "Ancient Mariner" (which I suppose the cut illustrates) about one who, having once looked round—

> walks on,
> And turns no more his head,
> Because he knows a frightful fiend
> Doth close behind him tread.

The other was a calendar, such as tradesmen often send. My brother paid no attention to this, but I looked at it after his death, and found that everything after September 18 had been torn out. You may be surprised at his having gone out alone the evening he was killed, but the fact is that during the last ten days or so of his life he had been quite free from the sense of being followed or watched.'

The end of the consultation was this. Harrington, who knew a neighbour of Karswell's, thought he saw a way of keeping a watch on his movements. It would be Dunning's part to be in readiness to try to cross Karswell's path at any moment, to keep the paper safe and in a place of ready access.

They parted. The next weeks were no doubt a severe strain upon Dunning's nerves: the intangible barrier which had seemed to rise about him on the day when he received the paper, gradually developed into a brooding blackness that cut him off from the means of escape to which one might have thought he might resort. No one was at hand who was likely to suggest them to him, and he seemed robbed of all initiative. He waited with inexpressible anxiety as May, June, and early July passed on, for a mandate from Harrington. But all this time Karswell remained immovable at Lufford.

At last, in less than a week before the date he had come to look upon as the end of his earthly activities, came a telegram: 'Leaves Victoria by boat train Thursday night. Do not miss. I come to you to-night. Harrington.'

He arrived accordingly, and they concocted plans. The train left Victoria at nine and its last stop before Dover was Croydon West. Harrington would mark down Karswell at Victoria, and look out for Dunning at Croydon, calling to him if need were by a name agreed upon. Dunning, disguised as far as might be, was to have no label or initials on any hand luggage, and must at all costs have the paper with him.

Dunning's suspense as he waited on the Croydon platform I need not attempt to describe. His sense of danger during the last days had only been sharpened by the fact that the cloud about him had perceptibly been lighter; but relief was an ominous symptom, and, if Karswell eluded him now, hope was gone: and there were so many chances of that. The rumour of the journey might be itself a device. The twenty minutes in which he paced the platform and persecuted every porter with inquiries as to the boat train were as bitter as any he had spent. Still, the train came, and Harrington was at the window. It was important, of course, that there should be no recognition: so Dunning got in at the farther end of the corridor carriage, and only gradually made his way to the compartment where Harrington and Karswell were. He was pleased, on the whole, to see that the train was far from full.

Karswell was on the alert, but gave no sign of recognition. Dunning took the seat not immediately facing him, and attempted, vainly at first, then with increasing command of his faculties, to reckon the possibilities of making the desired transfer. Opposite to Karswell, and next to Dunning, was a heap of Karswell's coats on the seat. It would be of no use to slip the paper into these—he would not be safe, or would not feel so, unless in some way it could be proffered by him and accepted by the other. There was a handbag, open, and with papers in it. Could he manage to conceal this (so that perhaps Karswell might leave the carriage without it), and then find and give it to him? This was the plan that suggested itself. If he could only have counselled with Harrington! but that could not be. The minutes went on. More than once Karswell rose and went out into the corridor. The second time Dunning was on the point of attempting to make the bag fall off the seat, but he caught Harrington's eye, and read in it a warning. Karswell, from the corridor, was watching: probably to see if the two men recognized each other. He returned, but was evidently restless: and, when he rose the third time, hope dawned, for something did slip off his seat and fall with hardly a sound to the floor. Karswell went out once more, and passed out of range of the corridor window. Dunning picked up what had fallen, and saw that the key was in his hands in the form of one of Cook's ticket-cases, with tickets in it. These cases have a pocket in the cover, and within very few seconds the paper of which we have heard was in the pocket of this one. To make the operation more secure, Harrington stood in the doorway of the compartment and fiddled with the blind. It was done, and done at the right time, for the train was now slowing down towards Dover.

In a moment more Karswell re-entered the compartment. As he did so, Dunning, managing, he knew not how, to suppress the tremble in his voice, handed him the ticket-case, saying, 'May I give you this, sir? I believe it is yours.' After a brief glance at the ticket inside, Karswell uttered the hoped-for response, 'Yes, it is; much obliged to you, sir,' and he placed it in his breast pocket.

Even in the few moments that remained—moments of tense anxiety, for they knew not to what a premature finding of the paper might lead—both men noticed that the carriage seemed to darken about them and to grow warmer; that Karswell was fidgety and oppressed; that he drew the heap of loose coats near to him and cast it back as if it repelled him; and that he then sat upright and glanced anxiously at both. They, with sickening anxiety, busied themselves in collecting their belongings; but they both thought that Karswell was on the point of speaking when the train stopped at Dover Town. It was natural that in the short space between town and pier they should both go into the corridor.

At the pier they got out, but so empty was the train that they were forced to linger on the platform until Karswell should have passed ahead of them with his porter on the way to the boat, and only then was it safe for them to exchange a pressure of the hand and a word of concentrated congratulation. The effect upon Dunning was to make him almost faint. Harrington made him lean up against the wall, while he himself went forward a few yards within sight of the gangway to the boat, at which Karswell had now arrived. The man at the head of it examined his ticket, and, laden with coats, he passed down into the boat. Suddenly the official called after him, 'You, sir, beg pardon, did the other gentleman show his ticket?' 'What the devil do you mean by the other gentleman?' Karswell's snarling voice called back from the deck. The man bent over and looked at him. 'The devil? Well, I don't know, I'm sure,' Harrington heard him say to himself, and then aloud, 'My mistake, sir; must have been your rugs! ask your pardon.' And then, to a subordinate near him, ''Ad he got a dog with him, or what? Funny thing: I could 'a' swore 'e wasn't alone. Well, whatever it was, they'll 'ave to see to it aboard. She's off now. Another week and we shall be gettin' the 'oliday customers.' In five minutes more there was nothing but the lessening lights of the boat, the long line of the Dover lamps, the night breeze, and the moon.

Long and long the two sat in their room at the 'Lord Warden'. In spite of the removal of their greatest anxiety, they were oppressed with a doubt, not of the lightest. Had they been justified in sending a man to his death, as they believed they had? Ought they not to warn him, at least? 'No,' said Harrington; 'if he is the murderer I think him, we have done no more than is just. Still, if you think it better—but how and where can you warn him?' 'He was booked to Abbeville only,' said Dunning. 'I saw that. If I wired to the hotels there in Joanne's Guide, "Examine your ticket-case, Dunning", I should feel happier. This is the 21st: he will have a day. But I am afraid he has gone into the dark.' So telegrams were left at the hotel office.

It is not clear whether these reached their destination, or whether, if they did, they were understood. All that is known is that, on the afternoon of the 23rd, an English traveller, examining the front of St. Wulfram's Church at Abbeville, then under extensive repair, was struck on the head and instantly killed by a stone falling from the scaffold erected round the north-western tower, there being, as was clearly proved, no workman on the scaffold at that moment: and the traveller's papers identified him as Mr. Karswell.

Only one detail shall be added. At Karswell's sale a set of Bewick, sold with all faults, was acquired by Harrington. The page with the woodcut of the traveller and the demon was, as he had expected, mutilated. Also, after a judicious interval, Harrington repeated to Dunning something of what he had heard his brother say in his sleep: but it was not long before Dunning stopped him.

W. SOMERSET MAUGHAM

Jane

I REMEMBER very well the occasion on which I first saw Jane Fowler. It is indeed only because the details of the glimpse I had of her then are so clear that I trust my recollection at all, for, looking back, I must confess that I find it hard to believe that it has not played me a fantastic trick. I had lately returned to London from China and was drinking a dish of tea with Mrs. Tower. Mrs. Tower had been seized with the prevailing passion for decoration; and, with the ruthlessness of her sex, had sacrificed chairs in which she had comfortably sat for years, tables, cabinets, ornaments on which her eyes had dwelt in peace since she was married, pictures that had been familiar to her for a generation; and delivered herself into the hands of an expert. Nothing remained in her drawing-room with which she had any association, or to which any sentiment was attached; and she had invited me that day to see the fashionable glory in which she now lived. Everything that could be pickled was pickled and what couldn't be pickled was painted. Nothing matched, but everything harmonized.

'Do you remember that ridiculous drawing-room suite that I used to have?' asked Mrs. Tower.

The curtains were sumptuous yet severe; the sofa was covered with Italian brocade; the chair on which I sat was in *petit point*. The room was beautiful, opulent without garishness and original without affectation; yet to me it lacked something; and while I praised with my lips I asked myself why I so much preferred the rather shabby chintz of the despised suite, the Victorian water-colours that I had known so long, and the ridiculous Dresden china that had adorned the chimney-piece. I wondered what it was that I missed in all these rooms that the decorators were turning out with a profitable industry. Was it heart? But Mrs. Tower looked about her happily.

'Don't you like my alabaster lamps?' she said. 'They give such a soft light.'

'Personally, I have a weakness for a light that you can see by,' I smiled.

'It's so difficult to combine that with a light that you can't be too much seen by,' laughed Mrs. Tower.

I had no notion what her age was. When I was quite a young man she was a married woman a good deal older than I, but now she treated me as her contemporary. She constantly said that she made no secret of her age, which was forty, and then added with a smile that all women took five years off. She never sought to conceal the fact that she dyed her hair (it was a very pretty brown with reddish tints), and she said she did this because hair was hideous while it was going grey; as soon as hers was white she would cease to dye it.

'Then they'll say what a young face I have.'

Meanwhile it was painted, though with discretion, and her eyes owed not a little of their vivacity to art. She was a handsome woman, exquisitely gowned, and in the sombre glow of the alabaster lamps did not look a day more than the forty she gave herself.

'It is only at my dressing-table that I can suffer the naked brightness of a thirty-two-candle electric bulb,' she added with smiling cynicism. 'There I need it to tell me first the hideous truth and then to enable me to take the necessary steps to correct it.'

We gossiped pleasantly about our common friends and Mrs. Tower brought me up to date in the scandal of the day. After roughing it here and there it was very agreeable to sit in a comfortable chair, the fire burning brightly on the hearth, charming tea-things set out on a charming table, and talk with this amusing, attractive woman. She treated me as a prodigal returned from his husks and was disposed to make much of me. She prided herself on her dinner-parties; she took no less trouble to have her guests suitably assorted than to give them excellent food; and there were few persons who did not look upon it as a treat to be bidden to one of them. Now she fixed a date and asked me whom I would like to meet.

'There's only one thing I must tell you. If Jane Fowler is still here I shall have to put it off.'

'Who is Jane Fowler?' I asked.

Mrs. Tower gave a rueful smile.

'Jane Fowler is my cross.'

'Oh!'

'Do you remember a photograph that I used to have on the piano before I had my room done, of a woman in a tight dress with tight sleeves and a gold locket, with her hair drawn back from a broad forehead and her ears showing and spectacles on a rather blunt nose? Well, that was Jane Fowler.'

'You had so many photographs about the room in your unregenerate days,' I said, vaguely.

'It makes me shudder to think of them. I've made them into a huge brown-paper parcel and hidden them in an attic.'

'Well, who is Jane Fowler?' I asked again, smiling.

'She's my sister-in-law. She was my husband's sister and she married a manufacturer in the North. She's been a widow for many years, and she's very well-to-do.'

'And why is she your cross?'

'She's worthy, she's dowdy, she's provincial. She looks twenty years older than I do and she's quite capable of telling any one she meets that we were at school together. She has an overwhelming sense of family affection and because I am her only living connexion she's devoted to me. When she comes to London it never occurs to her that she should stay anywhere but here—she thinks it would hurt my feelings—and she'll pay me visits of three or four weeks. We sit here and she knits and reads. And sometimes she insists on taking me to dine at Claridge's and she looks like a funny old charwoman and every one I particularly don't want to be seen by is sitting at the next table. When we are driving home she says she loves giving me a little treat. With her own hands she makes me tea-cosies that I am forced to use when she is here and doilies and centrepieces for the dining-room table.'

Mrs. Tower paused to take breath.

'I should have thought a woman of your tact would find a way to deal with a situation like that.'

'Ah, but don't you see, I haven't a chance. She's so immeasurably kind. She has a heart of gold. She bores me to death, but I wouldn't for anything let her suspect it.'

'And when does she arrive?'

'To-morrow.'

But the answer was hardly out of Mrs. Tower's mouth when the bell rang. There were sounds in the hall of a slight commotion and in a minute or two the butler ushered in an elderly lady.

'Mrs. Fowler,' he announced.

'Jane,' cried Mrs. Tower, springing to her feet. 'I wasn't expecting you to-day.'

'So your butler has just told me. I certainly said to-day in my letter.'

Mrs. Tower recovered her wits.

'Well, it doesn't matter. I'm very glad to see you whenever you come. Fortunately, I'm doing nothing this evening.'

'You mustn't let me give you any trouble. If I can have a boiled egg for my dinner that's all I shall want.'

A faint grimace for a moment distorted Mrs. Tower's handsome features. A boiled egg!

'Oh, I think we can do a little better than that.'

I chuckled inwardly when I recollected that the two ladies were contemporaries. Mrs. Fowler looked a good fifty-five. She was a rather big woman; she wore a black straw hat with a wide brim and from it a black lace veil hung over her shoulders, a cloak that oddly combined severity with fussiness, a long black dress, voluminous as though she wore several petticoats under it, and stout boots. She was evidently short-sighted, for she looked at you through large gold-rimmed spectacles.

'Won't you have a cup of tea?' asked Mrs. Tower.

'If it wouldn't be too much trouble. I'll take off my mantle.'

She began by stripping her hands of the black gloves she wore, and then took off her cloak. Round her neck was a solid gold chain from which hung a large gold locket in which I felt certain was a photograph of her deceased husband. Then she took off her hat and placed it neatly with her gloves and cloak on the sofa corner. Mrs. Tower pursed her lips. Certainly those garments did not go very well with the austere but sumptuous beauty of Mrs. Tower's redecorated drawing-room. I wondered where on earth Mrs. Fowler had found the extraordinary clothes she wore. They were not old and the materials were expensive. It was astounding to think that dressmakers still made things that had not been worn for a quarter of a century. Mrs. Fowler's grey hair was very plainly done, showing all her forehead and her ears, with a parting in the middle. It had evidently never known the tongs of Monsieur Marcel. Now her eyes fell on the tea-table with its teapot of Georgian silver and its cups in old Worcester.

'What have you done with the tea-cosy I gave you last time I came up, Marion?' she asked. 'Don't you use it?'

'Yes, I used it every day, Jane,' answered Mrs. Tower glibly. 'Unfortunately we had an accident with it a little while ago. It got burnt.'

'But the last one I gave you got burnt.'

'I'm afraid you'll think us very careless.'

'It doesn't really matter,' smiled Mrs. Fowler. 'I shall enjoy making you another. I'll go to Liberty's to-morrow and buy some silks.'

Mrs. Tower kept her face bravely.

'I don't deserve it, you know. Doesn't your vicar's wife need one?'

'Oh, I've just made her one,' said Mrs. Fowler brightly.

I noticed that when she smiled she showed white, small, and regular teeth. They were a real beauty. Her smile was certainly very sweet.

But I felt it high time for me to leave the two ladies to themselves, so I took my leave.

Early next morning Mrs. Tower rang me up and I heard at once from her voice that she was in high spirits.

'I've got the most wonderful news for you,' she said. 'Jane is going to be married.'

'Nonsense.'

'Her fiancé is coming to dine here to-night to be introduced to me and I want you to come too.'

'Oh, but I shall be in the way.'

'No, you won't. Jane suggested herself that I should ask you. Do come.'

She was bubbling over with laughter.

'Who is he?'

'I don't know. She tells me he's an architect. Can you imagine the sort of man Jane would marry?'

I had nothing to do and I could trust Mrs. Tower to give me a good dinner.

When I arrived Mrs. Tower, very splendid in a tea-gown a little too young for her, was alone.

'Jane is putting the finishing touches to her appearance. I'm longing for you to see her. She's all in a flutter. She says he adores her. His name is Gilbert and when she speaks of him her voice gets all funny and tremulous. It makes me want to laugh.'

'I wonder what he's like.'

'Oh, I'm sure I know. Very big and massive, with a bald head and an immense gold chain across an immense tummy. A large, fat, clean-shaven, red face and a booming voice.'

Mrs. Fowler came in. She wore a very stiff black silk dress with a wide skirt and a train. At the neck it was cut into a timid V and the sleeves came down to the elbows. She wore a necklace of diamonds set in silver. She carried in her hands a long pair of black gloves and a fan of black ostrich feathers. She managed (as so few people do) to look exactly what she was. You could never have thought her anything in the world but the respectable relict of a north-country manufacturer of ample means.

'You've really got quite a pretty neck, Jane,' said Mrs. Tower with a kindly smile.

It was indeed astonishingly young when you compared it with her weather-beaten face. It was smooth and unlined and the skin was white. And I noticed then that her head was very well placed on her shoulders.

'Has Marion told you my news?' she said, turning to me with that really charming smile of hers as if we were already old friends.

'I must congratulate you,' I said.

'Wait to do that till you've seen my young man.'

'I think it's too sweet to hear you talk of your young man,' smiled Mrs. Tower.

Mrs. Fowler's eyes certainly twinkled behind her preposterous spectacles.

'Don't expect any one too old. You wouldn't like me to marry a decrepit old gentleman with one foot in the grave, would you?'

This was the only warning she gave us. Indeed, there was no time for any further discussion, for the butler flung open the door and in a loud voice announced:

'Mr. Gilbert Napier.'

There entered a youth in a very well-cut dinner jacket. He was slight, not very tall, with fair hair in which there was a hint of a natural wave, clean-shaven and blue-eyed. He was not particularly good-looking, but he had a pleasant, amiable face. In ten years he would probably be wizened and sallow; but now, in extreme youth, he was fresh and clean and blooming. For he was certainly not more than twenty-four. My first thought was that this was the son of Jane Fowler's fiancé (I had not known he was a widower) come to say that his father was prevented from dining by a sudden attack of gout. But his eyes fell immediately on Mrs. Fowler, his face lit up, and he went towards her with both hands outstretched. Mrs. Fowler gave him hers, a demure smile on her lips, and turned to her sister-in-law.

'This is my young man, Marion,' she said.

He held out his hand.

'I hope you'll like me, Mrs. Tower,' he said. 'Jane tells me you're the only relation she has in the world.'

Mrs. Tower's face was wonderful to behold. I saw then to admiration how bravely good breeding and social usage could combat the instincts of the natural woman. For the astonishment and then the dismay that for an instant she could not conceal were quickly driven away, and her face assumed an expression of affable welcome. But she was evidently at a loss for words. It was not unnatural if Gilbert felt a certain embarrassment, and I was too busy preventing myself from laughing to think of anything to say. Mrs. Fowler alone kept perfectly calm.

'I know you'll like him, Marion. There's no one enjoys good food more than he does.' She turned to the young man. 'Marion's dinners are famous.'

'I know,' he beamed.

Mrs. Tower made some quick rejoinder and we went downstairs. I shall not soon forget the exquisite comedy of that meal. Mrs. Tower could not make up her mind whether the pair of them were playing a practical joke on her or whether Jane by wilfully concealing her fiancé's age had hoped to make her look foolish. But then Jane never jested and she was incapable of doing a malicious thing. Mrs. Tower was amazed, exasperated, and perplexed. But she had recovered her self-control, and for nothing would she have forgotten that she was a perfect hostess whose duty it was to make her party go. She talked vivaciously; but I wondered if Gilbert Napier saw how hard and vindictive was the expression of her eyes behind the mask of friendliness that she turned to him. She was measuring him. She was seeking to delve into the secret of his soul. I could see that she was in a passion, for under her rouge her cheeks glowed with an angry red.

'You've got a very high colour, Marion,' said Jane, looking at her amiably through her great round spectacles.

'I dressed in a hurry. I dare say I put on too much rouge.'

'Oh, is it rouge? I thought it was natural. Otherwise I shouldn't have mentioned it.' She gave Gilbert a shy little smile. 'You know, Marion and I were at school together. You would never think it to look at us now, would you? But of course I've lived a very quiet life.'

I do not know what she meant by these remarks; it was almost incredible that she made them in complete simplicity; but anyhow they goaded Mrs. Tower to such a fury that she flung her own vanity to the winds. She smiled brightly.

'We shall neither of us see fifty again, Jane,' she said.

If the observation was meant to discomfit the widow it failed.

'Gilbert says I mustn't acknowledge to more than forty-nine for his sake,' she answered blandly.

Mrs. Tower's hands trembled slightly, but she found a retort.

'There is of course a certain disparity of age between you,' she smiled.

'Twenty-seven years,' said Jane. 'Do you think it's too much? Gilbert says I'm very young for my age. I told you I shouldn't like to marry a man with one foot in the grave.'

I was really obliged to laugh and Gilbert laughed too. His laughter was frank and boyish. It looked as though he were amused at everything Jane said. But Mrs. Tower was almost at the end of her tether and I was afraid that unless relief came she would for once forget that she was a woman of the world. I came to the rescue as best I could.

'I suppose you're very busy buying your trousseau,' I said.

'No. I wanted to get my things from the dressmaker in Liverpool I've been to ever since I was first married. But Gilbert won't let me. He's very masterful, and of course he has wonderful taste.'

She looked at him with a little affectionate smile, demurely, as though she were a girl of seventeen.

Mrs. Tower went quite pale under her make-up.

'We're going to Italy for our honeymoon. Gilbert has never had a chance of studying Renaissance architecture and of course it's important for an architect to see things for himself. And we shall stop in Paris on the way and get my clothes there.'

'Do you expect to be away long?'

'Gilbert has arranged with his office to stay away for

six months. It will be such a treat for him, won't it? You see, he's never had more than a fortnight's holiday before.'

'Why not?' asked Mrs. Tower in a tone that no effort of will could prevent from being icy.

'He's never been able to afford it, poor dear.'

'Ah!' said Mrs. Tower, and into the exclamation put volumes.

Coffee was served and the ladies went upstairs. Gilbert and I began to talk in the desultory way in which men talk who have nothing whatever to say to one another; but in two minutes a note was brought in to me by the butler. It was from Mrs. Tower and ran as follows:

'Come upstairs quickly and then go as soon as you can. Take him with you. Unless I have it out with Jane at once I shall have a fit.'

I told a facile lie.

'Mrs. Tower has a headache and wants to go to bed. I think if you don't mind we'd better clear out.'

'Certainly,' he answered.

We went upstairs and five minutes later were on the doorstep. I called a taxi and offered the young man a lift.

'No, thanks,' he answered. 'I'll just walk to the corner and jump on a bus.'

Mrs. Tower sprang to the fray as soon as she heard the front-door close behind us.

'Are you crazy, Jane?' she cried.

'Not more than most people who don't habitually live in a lunatic asylum, I trust,' Jane answered blandly.

'May I ask why you're going to marry this young man?' asked Mrs. Tower with formidable politeness.

'Partly because he won't take no for an answer. He's asked me five times. I grew positively tired of refusing him.'

'And why do you think he's so anxious to marry you?'

'I amuse him.'

Mrs. Tower gave an exclamation of annoyance.

'He's an unscrupulous rascal. I very nearly told him so to his face.'

'You would have been wrong, and it wouldn't have been very polite.'

'He's penniless and you're rich. You can't be such a besotted fool as not to see that he's marrying you for your money.'

Jane remained perfectly composed. She observed her sister-in-law's agitation with detachment.

'I don't think he is, you know,' she replied. 'I think he's very fond of me.'

'You're an old woman, Jane.'

'I'm the same age as you are, Marion,' she smiled.

'I've never let myself go. I'm very young for my age. No one would think I was more than forty. But even I wouldn't dream of marrying a boy twenty years younger than myself.'

'Twenty-seven,' corrected Jane.

'Do you mean to tell me that you can bring yourself to believe that it's possible for a young man to care for a woman old enough to be his mother?'

'I've lived very much in the country for many years. I dare say there's a great deal about human nature that I don't know. They tell me there's a man called Freud, an Austrian, I believe . . .'

But Mrs. Tower interrupted her without any politeness at all.

'Don't be ridiculous, Jane. It's so undignified. It's so ungraceful. I always thought you were a sensible woman. Really, you're the last person I should ever have thought likely to fall in love with a boy.'

'But I'm not in love with him. I've told him that. Of course I like him very much or I wouldn't think of marrying him. I thought it only fair to tell him quite plainly what my feelings were towards him.'

Mrs. Tower gasped. The blood rushed to her head and her breathing oppressed her. She had no fan, but she seized the evening paper and vigorously fanned herself with it.

'If you're not in love with him why do you want to marry him?'

'I've been a widow a very long time and I've led a very quiet life. I thought I'd like a change.'

'If you want to marry just to be married why don't you marry a man of your own age?'

'No man of my own age has asked me five times. In fact, no man of my own age has asked me at all.'

Jane chuckled as she answered. It drove Mrs. Tower to the final pitch of frenzy.

'Don't laugh, Jane. I won't have it. I don't think you can be right in your mind. It's dreadful.'

It was altogether too much for her and she burst into tears. She knew that at her age it was fatal to cry, her eyes would be swollen for twenty-four hours and she would look a sight. But there was no help for it. She wept. Jane remained perfectly calm. She looked at Marion through her large spectacles and reflectively smoothed the lap of her black silk dress.

'You're going to be so dreadfully unhappy,' Mrs. Tower sobbed, dabbing her eyes cautiously in the hope that the black on her lashes would not smudge.

'I don't think so, you know,' Jane answered in those equable, mild tones of hers, as if there were a little smile behind the words. 'We've talked it over very thoroughly. I always think I'm a very easy person to live with. I think I shall make Gilbert very happy and comfortable. He's never had any one to look after him properly. We're only marrying after mature consideration. And we've decided that if either of us wants his liberty the other will place no obstacles in the way of his getting it.'

Mrs. Tower had by now recovered herself sufficiently to make a cutting remark.

'How much has he persuaded you to settle on him?'

'I wanted to settle a thousand a year on him, but he wouldn't hear of it. He was quite upset when I made the suggestion. He says he can earn quite enough for his own needs.'

'He's more cunning than I thought,' said Mrs. Tower acidly.

Jane paused a little and looked at her sister-in-law with kindly but resolute eyes.

'You see, my dear, it's different for you,' she said. 'You've never been so very much a widow, have you?'

Mrs. Tower looked at her. She blushed a little. She even felt slightly uncomfortable. But of course Jane was much too simple to intend an innuendo. Mrs. Tower gathered herself together with dignity.

'I'm so upset that I really must go to bed,' she said. 'We'll resume the conversation to-morrow morning.'

'I'm afraid that won't be very convenient, dear. Gilbert and I are going to get the licence to-morrow morning.'

Mrs. Tower threw up her hands in a gesture of dismay, but she found nothing more to say.

The marriage took place at a registrar's office. Mrs. Tower and I were the witnesses. Gilbert in a smart blue suit looked absurdly young and he was obviously nervous. It is a trying moment for any man. But Jane kept her admirable composure. She might have been in the habit of marrying as frequently as a woman of fashion. Only a slight colour on her cheeks suggested that beneath her calm was some faint excitement. It is a thrilling moment for any woman. She wore a very full dress of silver grey velvet in the cut of which I recognized the hand of the dressmaker in Liverpool (evidently a widow of unimpeachable character), who had made her gowns for so many years; but she had so far succumbed to the frivolity of the occasion as to wear a large picture hat covered with blue ostrich feathers. Her gold-rimmed spectacles made it extraordinarily grotesque. When the ceremony was over the registrar (somewhat taken aback, I thought, by the difference of age between the pair he was marrying) shook hands with her, tendering his strictly official congratulations; and the bridegroom, blushing slightly, kissed her. Mrs. Tower, resigned but implacable, kissed her; and then the bride looked at me expectantly. It was evidently fitting that I should kiss her too. I did. I confess that I felt a little shy as we walked out of the registrar's office past loungers who waited cynically to see the bridal pairs, and it was with relief that I stepped into Mrs. Tower's car. We drove to Victoria Station, for the happy couple were to go over to Paris by the two o'clock train, and Jane had insisted that the wedding-breakfast should be eaten at the station restaurant. She said it always made her nervous not to be on the platform in good time. Mrs. Tower, present only from a strong sense of family duty, was able to do little to make the party go off well; she ate nothing (for which I could not blame her, since the food was execrable, and anyway I hate champagne at luncheon) and talked in a strained voice. But Jane went through the menu conscientiously.

'I always think one should make a hearty meal before starting out on a journey,' she said.

We saw them off, and I drove Mrs. Tower back to her house.

'How long do you give it?' she said. 'Six months?'

'Let's hope for the best,' I smiled.

'Don't be so absurd. There can be no "best". You don't think he's marrying her for anything but her money, do you? Of course it can't last. My only hope is that she won't have to go through as much suffering as she deserves.'

I laughed. The charitable words were spoken in such a tone as to leave me in small doubt of Mrs. Tower's meaning.

'Well, if it doesn't last you'll have the consolation of saying: "I told you so,"' I said.

'I promise you I'll never do that.'

'Then you'll have the satisfaction of congratulating yourself on your self-control in not saying: "I told you so."'

'She's old and dowdy and dull.'

'Are you sure she's dull?' I said. 'It's true she doesn't

say very much, but when she says anything it's very much to the point.'

'I've never heard her make a joke in my life.'

I was once more in the Far East when Gilbert and Jane returned from their honeymoon, and this time I remained away for nearly two years. Mrs. Tower was a bad correspondent and though I sent her an occasional picture-postcard I received no news from her. But I met her within a week of my return to London; I was dining out and found that I was seated next to her. It was an immense party, I think we were four-and-twenty, like the blackbirds in the pie, and, arriving somewhat late, I was too confused by the crowd in which I found myself to notice who was there. But when we sat down, looking round the long table I saw that a good many of my fellow guests were well known to the public from their photographs in the illustrated papers. Our hostess had a weakness for the persons technically known as celebrities and this was an unusually brilliant gathering. When Mrs. Tower and I had exchanged the conventional remarks that two people make when they have not seen one another for a couple of years I asked about Jane.

'She's very well,' said Mrs. Tower with a certain dryness.

'How has the marriage turned out?'

Mrs. Tower paused a little and took a salted almond from the dish in front of her.

'It appears to be quite a success.'

'You were wrong then?'

'I said it wouldn't last and I still say it won't last. It's contrary to human nature.'

'Is she happy?'

'They're both happy.'

'I suppose you don't see very much of them.'

'At first I saw quite a lot of them. But now . . .' Mrs. Tower pursed her lips a little. 'Jane is becoming very grand.'

'What *do* you mean?' I laughed.

'I think I should tell you that she's here to-night.'

'Here?'

I was startled. I looked round the table again. Our hostess was a delightful and an entertaining woman, but I could not imagine that she would be likely to invite to a dinner such as this the elderly and dowdy wife of an obscure architect. Mrs. Tower saw my perplexity and was shrewd enough to see what was in my mind. She smiled thinly.

'Look on the left of our host.'

I looked. Oddly enough, the woman who sat there had by her fantastic appearance attracted my attention the moment I was ushered into the crowded drawing-room. I thought I noticed a gleam of recognition in her eye, but to the best of my belief I had never seen her before. She was not a young woman, for her hair was iron-grey; it was cut very short and clustered thickly round her well-shaped head in tight curls. She made no attempt at youth, for she was conspicuous in that gathering by using neither lipstick, rouge, nor powder. Her face, not a particularly handsome one, was red and weather-beaten; but because it owed nothing to artifice had a naturalness that was very pleasing. It contrasted oddly with the whiteness of her shoulders. They were really magnificent. A woman of thirty might have been proud of them. But her dress was extraordinary. I had not seen often anything more audacious. It was cut very low, with short skirts, which were then the fashion, in black and yellow; it had almost the effect of fancy dress and yet so became her that though on any one else it would have been outrageous, on her it had the inevitable simplicity of nature. And to complete the impression of an eccentricity in which there was no pose and of an extravagance in which there was no ostentation she wore, attached by a broad black ribbon, a single eye-glass.

'You're not going to tell me *that* is your sister-in-law,' I gasped.

'That is Jane Napier,' said Mrs. Tower icily.

At that moment she was speaking. Her host was turned towards her with an anticipatory smile. A baldish white-haired man, with a sharp, intelligent face, who sat on her left, was leaning forward eagerly, and the couple who sat opposite, ceasing to talk with one another, listened intently. She said her say and they all, with a sudden movement, threw themselves back in their chairs and burst into vociferous laughter. From the other side of the table a man addressed Mrs. Tower: I recognized a famous statesman.

'Your sister-in-law has made another joke, Mrs. Tower,' he said.

Mrs. Tower smiled.

'She's priceless, isn't she?'

'Let me have a long drink of champagne and then for heaven's sake tell me all about it,' I said.

Well, this is how I gathered it had all happened. At the beginning of their honeymoon Gilbert took Jane to various dressmakers in Paris and he made no objection to her choosing a number of 'gowns' after her own heart; but he persuaded her to have a 'frock' or two made according to his own design. It appeared that he had a knack for that kind of work. He engaged a smart French maid. Jane had never had such a thing before. She did her own mending and when she wanted 'doing up' was in the habit of ringing for the housemaid. The dresses Gilbert had devised were very different from anything she had worn before; but he had been careful not to go too far too quickly, and because it pleased him she persuaded herself, though not without misgivings, to wear them in preference to those she had chosen herself. Of course she could not wear them with the voluminous petticoats she had been in the habit of using, and these, though it cost her an anxious moment, she discarded.

'Now, if you please,' said Mrs. Tower, with something very like a sniff of disapproval, 'she wears nothing but thin silk tights. It's a wonder to me she doesn't catch her death of cold at her age.'

Gilbert and the French maid taught her how to wear her clothes, and, unexpectedly enough, she was very quick at learning. The French maid was in raptures over Madame's arms and shoulders. It was a scandal not to show anything so fine.

'Wait a little, Alphonsine,' said Gilbert. 'The next lot of clothes I design for Madame we'll make the most of her.'

The spectacles of course were dreadful. No one could look really well in gold-rimmed spectacles. Gilbert tried some with tortoise-shell rims. He shook his head.

'They'd look all right on a girl,' he said. 'You're too old to wear spectacles, Jane.' Suddenly he had an inspiration. 'By George, I've got it. You must wear an eyeglass.'

'Oh, Gilbert, I couldn't.'

She looked at him, and his excitement, the excitement of the artist, made her smile. He was so sweet to her she wanted to do what she could to please him.

'I'll try,' she said.

When they went to an optician and, suited with the right size, she placed an eye-glass jauntily in her eye Gilbert clapped his hands. There and then, before the astonished shopman, he kissed her on both cheeks.

'You look wonderful,' he cried.

So they went down to Italy and spent happy months studying Renaissance and Baroque architecture. Jane not only grew accustomed to her changed appearance, but found she liked it. At first she was a little shy when she went into the dining-room of an hotel and people turned round to stare at her, no one had ever raised an eyelid to look at her before, but presently she found that the sensation was not disagreeable. Ladies came up to her and asked her where she got her dress.

'Do you like it?' she answered demurely. 'My husband designed it for me.'

'I should like to copy it if you don't mind.'

Jane had certainly for many years lived a very quiet life, but she was by no means lacking in the normal instincts of her sex. She had her answer ready.

'I'm so sorry, but my husband's very particular and he won't hear of any one copying my frocks. He wants me to be unique.'

She had an idea that people would laugh when she said this, but they didn't; they merely answered:

'Oh, of course I quite understand. You *are* unique.'

But she saw them making mental notes of what she wore, and for some reason this quite 'put her about'. For once in her life that she wasn't wearing what everybody else did, she reflected, she didn't see why everybody else should want to wear what she did.

'Gilbert,' she said, quite sharply for her, 'next time you're designing dresses for me I wish you'd design things that people *can't* copy.'

'The only way to do that is to design things that only you can wear.'

'Can't you do that?'

'Yes, if you'll do something for me.'

'What is it?'

'Cut off your hair.'

I think this was the first time that Jane jibbed. Her hair was long and thick and as a girl she had been quite vain of it; to cut it off was a very drastic proceeding. This really was burning her boats behind her. In her case it was not the first step that cost so much, it was the last; but she took it ('I know Marion will think me a perfect fool, and I shall *never* be able to go to Liverpool again,' she said), and when they passed through Paris on their way home Gilbert led her (she felt quite sick, her heart was beating so fast) to the best hairdresser in the world. She came out of his shop with a jaunty, saucy, impudent head of crisp grey curls. Pygmalion had finished his fantastic masterpiece: Galatea was come to life.

'Yes,' I said, 'but that isn't enough to explain why Jane is here to-night amid this crowd of duchesses, cabinet ministers, and such-like; nor why she is sitting on one side of her host with an Admiral of the Fleet on the other.'

'Jane is a humorist,' said Mrs. Tower. 'Didn't you see them all laughing at what she said?'

There was no doubt now of the bitterness in Mrs. Tower's heart.

'When Jane wrote and told me they were back from their honeymoon I thought I must ask them both to dinner. I didn't much like the idea, but I felt it had to be done. I knew the party would be deadly and I wasn't going to sacrifice any of the people who really mattered. On the other hand, I didn't want Jane to think I hadn't any nice friends. You know I never have more than eight, but on this occasion I thought it would make things go better if I had twelve. I'd been too busy to see Jane until the evening of the party. She kept us all waiting a little—that was Gilbert's cleverness—and at last she sailed in. You could have knocked me down with a feather. She made the rest of the women look dowdy and provincial. She made me feel like a painted old trollop.'

Mrs. Tower drank a little champagne.

'I wish I could describe the frock to you. It would have been quite impossible on any one else; on her it was perfect. And the eye-glass! I'd known her for thirty-five years and I'd never seen her without spectacles.'

'But you knew she had a good figure.'

'How should I? I'd never seen her except in the clothes you first saw her in. Did *you* think she had a good figure? She seemed not to be unconscious of the sensation she made but to take it as a matter of course. I thought of my dinner and I heaved a sigh of relief. Even if she was a little heavy in hand, with that appearance it didn't so very much matter. She was sitting at the other end of the table and I heard a good deal of laughter, I was glad to think that the other people were playing up well; but after dinner I was a good deal taken aback when no less than three men came up to me and told me that my sister-in-law was priceless, and did I think she would allow them to call on her? I didn't quite know whether I was standing on my head or my heels. Twenty-four hours later our hostess of to-night rang me up and said she had heard my sister-in-law was in London and she was priceless and would I ask her to luncheon to meet her? She has an infallible instinct, that woman: in a month every one was talking about Jane. I am here to-night, not because I've known our hostess for twenty years and have asked her to dinner a hundred times, but because I'm Jane's sister-in-law.'

Poor Mrs. Tower. The position was galling, and though I could not help being amused, for the tables were turned on her with a vengeance, I felt that she deserved my sympathy.

'People never can resist those who make them laugh,' I said, trying to console her.

'She never makes *me* laugh.'

Once more from the top of the table I heard a guffaw and guessed that Jane had said another amusing thing.

'Do you mean to say that you are the only person who doesn't think her funny?' I asked, smiling.

'Had it struck *you* that she was a humorist?'

'I'm bound to say it hadn't.'

'She says just the same things as she's said for the last thirty-five years. I laugh when I see every one else does because I don't want to seem a perfect fool, but I am not amused.'

'Like Queen Victoria,' I said.

It was a foolish jest and Mrs. Tower was quite right sharply to tell me so. I tried another tack.

'Is Gilbert here?' I asked, looking down the table.

'Gilbert was asked because she won't go out without

him, but to-night he's at a dinner of the Architects' Institute or whatever it's called.'

'I'm dying to renew my acquaintance with her.'

'Go and talk to her after dinner. She'll ask you to her Tuesdays.'

'Her Tuesdays?'

'She's at home every Tuesday evening. You'll meet there every one you ever heard of. They're the best parties in London. She's done in one year what I've failed to do in twenty.'

'But what you tell me is really miraculous. How has it been done?'

Mrs. Tower shrugged her handsome but adipose shoulders.

'I shall be glad if you'll tell me,' she replied.

After dinner I tried to make my way to the sofa on which Jane was sitting, but I was intercepted and it was not till a little later that my hostess came up to me and said:

'I must introduce you to the star of my party. Do you know Jane Napier? She's priceless. She's much more amusing than your comedies.'

I was taken up to the sofa. The admiral who had been sitting beside her at dinner was with her still. He showed no sign of moving and Jane, shaking hands with me, introduced me to him.

'Do you know Sir Reginald Frobisher?'

We began to chat. It was the same Jane as I had known before, perfectly simple, homely, and unaffected, but her fantastic appearance certainly gave a peculiar savour to what she said. Suddenly I found myself shaking with laughter. She had made a remark, sensible and to the point, but not in the least witty, which her manner of saying and the bland look she gave me through her eye-glass made perfectly irresistible. I felt light-hearted and buoyant. When I left her she said to me:

'If you've got nothing better to do, come and see us on Tuesday evening. Gilbert will be so glad to see you.'

'When he's been a month in London he'll know that he *can* have nothing better to do,' said the admiral.

So, on Tuesday but rather late, I went to Jane's. I confess I was a little surprised at the company. It was quite a remarkable collection of writers, painters, and politicians, actors, great ladies, and great beauties: Mrs. Tower was right, it was a grand party; I had seen nothing like it in London since Stafford House was sold. No particular entertainment was provided. The refreshments were adequate without being luxurious. Jane in her quiet way seemed to be enjoying herself; I could not see that she took a great deal of trouble with her guests, but they seemed to like being there, and the gay, pleasant party did not break up till two in the morning. After that I saw much of her. I not only went often to her house, but seldom went out to luncheon or to dinner without meeting her. I am an amateur of humour and I sought to discover in what lay her peculiar gift. It was impossible to repeat anything she said, for the fun, like certain wines, would not travel. She had no gift for epigram. She never made a brilliant repartee. There was no malice in her remarks nor sting in her rejoinders. There are those who think that impropriety, rather than brevity, is the soul of wit; but she never said a thing that could have brought a blush to a Victorian cheek. I think her humour was unconscious and I am sure it was unpremeditated. It flew like a butterfly from flower to flower, obedient only to its own caprice and pursuant of neither method nor intention. It depended on the way she spoke and on the way she looked. Its subtlety gained by the flaunting and extravagant appearance that Gilbert had achieved for her; but her appearance was only an element in it. Now of course she was the fashion and people laughed if she but opened her mouth. They no longer wondered that Gilbert had married a wife so much older than himself. They saw that Jane was a woman with whom age did not count. They thought him a devilish lucky young fellow. The admiral quoted Shakespeare to me: 'Age cannot wither her, nor custom stale her infinite variety.' Gilbert was delighted with her success. As I came to know him better I grew to like him. It was quite evident that he was neither a rascal nor a fortune-hunter. He was not only immensely proud of Jane but genuinely devoted to her. His kindness to her was touching. He was a very unselfish and sweet-tempered young man.

'Well, what do you think of Jane now?' he said to me once, with boyish triumph.

'I don't know which of you is more wonderful,' I said. 'You or she.'

'Oh, I'm nothing.'

'Nonsense. You don't think I'm such a fool as not to see that it's you, and you only, who've made Jane what she is.'

'My only merit is that I saw what was there when it wasn't obvious to the naked eye,' he answered.

'I can understand your seeing that she had in her the possibility of that remarkable appearance, but how in the world have you made her into a humorist?'

'But I always thought the things she said a perfect scream. She was always a humorist.'

'You're the only person who ever thought so.'

Mrs. Tower, not without magnanimity, acknowledged that she had been mistaken in Gilbert. She grew quite attached to him. But notwithstanding appearances she never faltered in her opinion that the marriage could not last. I was obliged to laugh at her.

'Why, I've never seen such a devoted couple,' I said.

'Gilbert is twenty-seven now. It's just the time for a pretty girl to come along. Did you notice the other evening at Jane's that pretty little niece of Sir Reginald's? I thought Jane was looking at them both with a good deal of attention, and I wondered to myself.'

'I don't believe Jane fears the rivalry of any girl under the sun.'

'Wait and see,' said Mrs. Tower.

'You gave it six months.'

'Well, now I give it three years.'

When any one is very positive in an opinion it is only human nature to wish him proved wrong. Mrs. Tower was really too cocksure. But such a satisfaction was not mine, for the end that she had always and confidently predicted to the ill-assorted match did in point of fact come. Still, the fates seldom give us what we want in the way we want it, and though Mrs. Tower could flatter herself that she had been right, I think after all she would sooner have been wrong. For things did not happen at all in the way she expected.

One day I received an urgent message from her and fortunately went to see her at once. When I was shown into the room Mrs. Tower rose from her chair and came towards me with the stealthy swiftness of a leopard stalking his prey. I saw that she was excited.

'Jane and Gilbert have separated,' she said.

'Not really? Well, you were right after all.'

Mrs. Tower looked at me with an expression I could not understand.

'Poor Jane,' I muttered.

'Poor Jane!' she repeated, but in tones of such derision that I was dumbfounded.

She found some difficulty in telling me exactly what had occurred.

Gilbert had left her a moment before she leaped to the telephone to summon me. When he entered the room, pale and distraught, she saw at once that something terrible had happened. She knew what he was going to say before he said it.

'Marion, Jane has left me.'

She gave him a little smile and took his hand.

'I knew you'd behave like a gentleman. It would have been dreadful for her for people to think that *you* had left her.'

'I've come to you because I knew I could count on your sympathy.'

'Oh, I don't blame you, Gilbert,' said Mrs. Tower, very kindly. 'It was bound to happen.'

He sighed.

'I suppose so. I couldn't hope to keep her always. She was too wonderful and I'm a perfectly commonplace fellow.'

Mrs. Tower patted his hand. He was really behaving beautifully.

'And what is going to happen now?'

'Well, she's going to divorce me.'

'Jane always said she'd put no obstacle in your way if ever you wanted to marry a girl.'

'You don't think it's likely I should ever be willing to marry any one else after being Jane's husband,' he answered.

Mrs. Tower was puzzled.

'Of course you mean that *you've* left Jane.'

'I? That's the last thing I should ever do.'

'Then why is she divorcing you?'

'She's going to marry Sir Reginald Frobisher as soon as the decree is made absolute.'

Mrs. Tower positively screamed. Then she felt so faint that she had to get her smelling salts

'After all you've done for her?'

'I've done nothing for her.'

'Do you mean to say you're going to allow yourself to be made use of like that?'

'We arranged before we married that if either of us wanted his liberty the other should put no hindrance in the way.'

'But that was done on your account. Because you were twenty-seven years younger than she was.'

'Well, it's come in very useful for her,' he answered bitterly.

Mrs. Tower expostulated, argued, and reasoned; but Gilbert insisted that no rules applied to Jane, and he must do exactly what she wanted. He left Mrs. Tower prostrate. It relieved her a good deal to give me a full account of this interview. It pleased her to see that I was as surprised as herself and if I was not so indignant with Jane as she was she ascribed that to the criminal lack of morality incident to my sex. She was still in a state of extreme agitation when the door was opened and the butler showed in—Jane herself. She was dressed in black and white as no doubt befitted her slightly ambiguous position, but in a dress so original and fantastic, in a hat so striking, that I positively gasped at the sight of her. But she was as ever bland and collected. She came forward to kiss Mrs. Tower, but Mrs. Tower withdrew herself with icy dignity.

'Gilbert has been here,' she said.

'Yes, I know,' smiled Jane. 'I told him to come and see you. I'm going to Paris to-night and I want you to be very kind to him while I am away. I'm afraid just at first he'll be rather lonely and I shall feel more comfortable if I can count on your keeping an eye on him.'

Mrs. Tower clasped her hands.

'Gilbert has just told me something that I can hardly bring myself to believe. He tells me that you're going to divorce him to marry Reginald Frobisher.'

'Don't you remember, before I married Gilbert you advised me to marry a man of my own age. The admiral is fifty-three.'

'But, Jane, you owe everything to Gilbert,' said Mrs. Tower indignantly. 'You wouldn't exist without him. Without him to design your clothes, you'll be nothing.'

'Oh, he's promised to go on designing my clothes,' Jane answered blandly.

'No woman could want a better husband. He's always been kindness itself to you.'

'Oh, I know he's been sweet.'

'How *can* you be so heartless?'

'But I was never in love with Gilbert,' said Jane. 'I always told him that. I'm beginning to feel the need of the companionship of a man of my own age. I think I've probably been married to Gilbert long enough.

The young have no conversation.' She paused a little and gave us both a charming smile. 'Of course I shan't lose sight of Gilbert. I've arranged that with Reginald. The admiral has a niece that would just suit him. As soon as we're married we'll ask them to stay with us at Malta—you know that the admiral is to have the Mediterranean Command—and I shouldn't be at all surprised if they fell in love with one another.'

Mrs. Tower gave a little sniff.

'And have you arranged with the admiral that if you want your liberty neither should put any hindrance in the way of the other?'

'I suggested it,' Jane answered with composure. 'But the admiral says he knows a good thing when he sees it and he won't want to marry any one else, and if any one wants to marry me—he has eight twelve-inch guns on his flagship and he'll discuss the matter at short range.' She gave us a look through her eye-glass which even the fear of Mrs. Tower's wrath could not prevent me from laughing at. 'I think the admiral's a very passionate man.'

Mrs. Tower indeed gave me an angry frown.

'I never thought you funny, Jane,' she said. 'I never understood why people laughed at the things you said.'

'I never thought I was funny myself, Marion,' smiled Jane, showing her bright, regular teeth. 'I am glad to leave London before too many people come round to our opinion.'

'I wish you'd tell me the secret of your astonishing success,' I said.

She turned to me with that bland, homely look I knew so well.

'You know, when I married Gilbert and settled in

London and people began to laugh at what I said no one was more surprised than I was. I'd said the same things for thirty years and no one ever saw anything to laugh at. I thought it must be my clothes or my bobbed hair or my eyeglass. Then I discovered it was because I spoke the truth. It was so unusual that people thought it humorous. One of these days some one else will discover the secret, and when people habitually tell the truth of course there'll be nothing funny in it.'

'And why am I the only person not to think it funny?' asked Mrs. Tower.

Jane hesitated a little as though she were honestly searching for a satisfactory explanation.

'Perhaps you don't know the truth when you see it, Marion dear,' she answered in her mild, good-natured way.

It certainly gave her the last word. I felt that Jane would always have the last word. She *was* priceless.

LEONARD MERRICK

The Judgement of Paris

In the summer of the memorable year ——, but the date doesn't matter, Robichon and Quinquart both paid court to Mademoiselle Brouette. Mademoiselle Brouette was a captivating actress, Robichon and Quinquart were the most comic of comedians, and all three were members of the Théâtre Suprême.

Robichon was such an idol of the public's that they used to laugh before he uttered the first word of his role; and Quinquart was so vastly popular that his silence threw the audience into convulsions.

Professional rivalry apart, the two were good friends, although they were suitors for the same lady, and this was doubtless due to the fact that the lady favoured the robust Robichon no more than she favoured the skinny Quinquart. She flirted with them equally, she approved them equally—and at last, when each of them had plagued her beyond endurance, she promised in a pet that she would marry the one that was the better actor.

Tiens! Not a player on the stage, not a critic on the Press could quite make up his mind which the better actor was. Only Suzanne Brouette could have said anything so tantalizing.

'But how shall we decide the point, Suzanne?' stammered Robichon helplessly. 'Whose pronouncement will you accept?'

'How can the question be settled?' queried Quinquart, dismayed. 'Who shall be the judge?'

'Paris shall be the judge,' affirmed Suzanne. 'We are

the servants of the public—I will take the public's word!'

Of course she was as pretty as a picture, or she couldn't have done these things.

Then poor Quinquart withdrew, plunged in reverie. So did Robichon. Quinquart reflected that she had been talking through her expensive hat. Robichon was of the same opinion. The public lauded them both, was no less generous to one than to the other—to wait for the judgement of Paris appeared equivalent to postponing the matter *sine die*. No way out presented itself to Quinquart. None occurred to Robichon.

'Mon vieux,' said the latter, as they sat on the terrace of their favourite café a day or two before the annual vacation, 'let us discuss this amicably. Have a cigarette! You are an actor, therefore you consider yourself more talented than I. I, too, am an actor, therefore I regard you as less gifted than myself. So much for our artistic standpoints! But we are also men of the world, and it must be obvious to both of us that we might go on being funny until we reached our death-beds without demonstrating the supremacy of either. Enfin, our only hope lies in versatility—the conqueror must distinguish himself in a solemn part!' He viewed the other with complacence, for the quaint Quinquart had been designed for a droll by Nature.

'Right!' said Quinquart. He contemplated his colleague with satisfaction, for it was impossible to fancy the fat Robichon in tragedy.

'I perceive only one drawback to the plan,' continued Robichon, 'the Management will never consent to accord us a chance. Is it not always so in the theatre? One succeeds in a certain line of business and one must be resigned to play that line as long as one lives. If my earliest success had been scored as a villain of melodrama, it would be believed that I was competent to enact nothing but villains of melodrama; it happened that I made a hit as a comedian, wherefore nobody will credit that I am capable of anything but being comic.'

'Same here!' concurred Quinquart. 'Well, then, what do you propose?'

Robichon mused. 'Since we shall not be allowed to do ourselves justice on the stage, we must find an opportunity off it!'

'A private performance? Good! Yet, if it is a private performance, how is Paris to be the judge?'

'Ah,' murmured Robichon, 'that is certainly a stumbling-block.'

They sipped their apéritifs moodily. Many heads were turned towards the little table where they sat. 'There are Quinquart and Robichon, how amusing they always are!' said passers-by, little guessing the anxiety at the laughter-makers' hearts.

'What's to be done?' sighed Quinquart at last.

Robichon shrugged his fat shoulders, with a frown.

Both were too absorbed to notice that, after a glance of recognition, one of the pedestrians had paused, and was still regarding them irresolutely. He was a tall, burly man, habited in rusty black, and the next moment, as if finding courage, he stepped forward and spoke:

'Gentlemen, I ask pardon for the liberty I take—impulse urges me to seek your professional advice! I am in a position to pay a moderate fee. Will you permit me to explain myself?'

'Monsieur,' returned Robichon, 'we are in deep consideration of our latest parts. We shall be pleased to give you our attention at some other time.'

'Alas!' persisted the new-comer, 'with me time presses. I, too, am considering my latest part—and it will be the only speaking part I have ever played, though I have been "appearing" for twenty years.'

'What? You have been a super for twenty years?' said Quinquart, with a grimace.

'No, monsieur,' replied the stranger grimly. 'I have been the Public Executioner; and I am going to lecture on the horrors of the post I have resigned.'

The two comedians stared at him aghast. Across the sunlit terrace seemed to have fallen the black shadow of the guillotine.

'I am Jacques Roux,' the man went on. 'I am "trying it on the dog" at Appeville-sous-Bois next week, and I have what you gentlemen call "stage fright"—I, who never knew what nervousness meant before! Is it not queer? As often as I rehearse walking on to the platform, I feel myself to be all arms and legs—I don't know what to do with them. Formerly, I scarcely remembered my arms and legs; but, of course, my attention used to be engaged by the other fellow's head. Well, it struck me that you might consent to give me a few hints in deportment. Probably one lesson would suffice.'

'Sit down,' said Robichon. 'Why did you abandon your official position?'

'Because I awakened to the truth,' Roux answered. 'I no longer agree with capital punishment; it is a crime that should be abolished.'

'The scruples of conscience, hein?'

'That is it.'

'Fine!' said Robichon. 'What dramatic lines such a lecture might contain! And of what is it to consist?'

'It is to consist of the history of my life—my youth, my poverty, my experiences as Executioner, and my remorse.'

'Magnificent!' said Robichon. 'The spectres of your victims pursue you even to the platform. Your voice fails you, your eyes start from your head in terror. You gasp for mercy—and imagination splashes your outstretched hands with gore. The audience thrill, women swoon, strong men are breathless with emotion.' Suddenly he smote the table with his big fist, and little Quinquart nearly fell off his chair, for he divined the inspiration of his rival. 'Listen!' cried Robichon, 'are you known at Appeville-sous-Bois?'

'My name is known, yes.'

'Bah! I mean are you known personally, have you acquaintances there?'

'Oh, no. But why?'

'There will be nobody to recognize you?'

'It is very unlikely in such a place.'

'What do you estimate that your profits will amount to?'

'It is only a small hall, and the prices are cheap. Perhaps two hundred and fifty francs.'

'And you are nervous, you would like to postpone your début?'

'I should not be sorry, I admit. But, again, why?'

'I will tell you why—I offer you five hundred francs to let me take your place!'

'Monsieur!'

'Is it a bargain?'

'I do not understand!'

'I have a whim to figure in a solemn part. You can explain next day that you missed your train—that you were ill, there are a dozen explanations that can be made; you will not be supposed to know that I personated you—the responsibility for that is mine. What do you say?'

'It is worth double the money,' demurred the man.

'Not a bit of it! All the Press will shout the story of my practical joke—Paris will be astounded that I, Robichon, lectured as Jacques Roux and curdled an audience's blood. Millions will speak of your intended lecture tour who otherwise would never have heard of it. I am giving you the grandest advertisement, and paying you for it, besides. Enfin, I will throw a deportment lesson in! Is it agreed?'

'Agreed, monsieur!' said Roux.

Oh, the trepidation of Quinquart! Who could eclipse Robichon if his performance of the part equalled his conception of it? At the theatre that evening Quinquart followed Suzanne about the wings pathetically. He was garbed like a buffoon, but he felt like Romeo. The throng that applauded his capers were far from suspecting the romantic longings under his magenta wig. For the first time in his life he was thankful that the author hadn't given him more to do.

And, oh, the excitement of Robichon! He was to put his powers to a tremendous test, and if he made the effect that he anticipated he had no fear of Quinquart's going one better. Suzanne, to whom he whispered his project proudly, announced an intention of being present to 'see the fun'. Quinquart also promised to be there. Robichon sat up all night preparing his lecture.

If you wish to know whether Suzanne rejoiced at the

prospect of his winning her, history is not definite on the point; but some chroniclers assert that at this period she made more than usual of Quinquart, who had developed a hump as big as the Panthéon.

And they all went to Appeville-sous-Bois.

Though no one in the town was likely to know the features of the Executioner, it was to be remembered that people there might know the actor's, and Robichon had made up to resemble Roux as closely as possible. Arriving at the humble hall, he was greeted by the lessee, heard that a 'good house' was expected, and smoked a cigarette in the retiring-room while the audience assembled.

At eight o'clock the lessee reappeared.

'All is ready, Monsieur Roux,' he said.

Robichon rose.

He saw Suzanne and Quinquart in the third row, and was tempted to wink at them.

'Ladies and gentlemen——'

All eyes were riveted on him as he began; even the voice of the 'Executioner' exercised a morbid fascination over the crowd. The men nudged their neighbours appreciatively, and women gazed at him, half horrified, half charmed.

The opening of his address was quiet enough—there was even a humorous element in it, as he narrated imaginary experiences of his boyhood. People tittered, and then glanced at one another with an apologetic air, as if shocked at such a monster's daring to amuse them. Suzanne whispered to Quinquart: 'Too cheerful; he hasn't struck the right note.' Quinquart whispered back gloomily: 'Wait; he may be playing for the contrast!'

And Quinquart's assumption was correct. Gradually

the cheerfulness faded from the speaker's voice, the humorous incidents were past. Gruesome, hideous, grew the anecdotes. The hall shivered. Necks were craned, and white faces twitched suspensively. He dwelt on the agonies of the Condemned, he recited crimes in detail, he mirrored the last moments before the blade fell. He shrieked his remorse, his lacerating remorse. 'I am a murderer,' he sobbed; and in the hall one might have heard a pin drop.

There was no applause when he finished—that set the seal on his success; he bowed and withdrew amid tense silence. Still none moved in the hall, until, with a rush, the representatives of the Press sped forth to proclaim Jacques Roux an unparalleled sensation.

The triumph of Robichon! How generous were the congratulations of Quinquart, and how sweet the admiring tributes of Suzanne! And there was another compliment to come—nothing less than a card from the Marquis de Thevenin, requesting an interview at his home.

'Ah!' exclaimed Robichon, enravished, 'an invitation from a noble! That proves the effect I made, hein?'

'Who may he be?' inquired Quinquart. 'I never heard of the Marquis de Thevenin!'

'It is immaterial whether you have heard of him,' replied Robichon. 'He is a marquis, and he desires to converse with me! It is an honour that one must appreciate. I shall assuredly go.'

And, being a bit of a snob, he sought a fiacre in high feather.

The drive was short, and when the cab stopped he was distinctly taken aback to perceive the unpretentious aspect of the nobleman's abode. It was, indeed, nothing better than a lodging. A peasant admitted him, and the room to which he was ushered boasted no warmer hospitality than a couple of candles and a decanter of wine. However, the sconces were massive silver. Monsieur le marquis, he was informed, had been suddenly compelled to summon his physician, and begged that Monsieur Roux would allow him a few minutes' grace.

Robichon ardently admired the candlesticks, but began to think he might have supped more cosily with Suzanne.

It was a long time before the door opened.

The Marquis de Thevenin was old—so old that he seemed to be falling to pieces as he tottered forward. His skin was yellow and shrivelled, his mouth sunken, his hair sparse and grey; and from this weird face peered strange eyes—the eyes of a fanatic.

'Monsieur, I owe you many apologies for my delay,' he wheezed. 'My unaccustomed exertion this evening fatigued me, and on my return from the hall I found it necessary to see my doctor. Your lecture was wonderful, Monsieur Roux—most interesting and instructive; I shall never forget it.'

Robichon bowed his acknowledgements.

'Sit down, Monsieur Roux, do not stand! Let me offer you some wine. I am forbidden to touch it myself. I am a poor host, but my age must be my excuse.'

'To be the guest of monsieur le marquis,' murmured Robichon, 'is a privilege, an honour, which—er——'

'Ah,' sighed the marquis. 'I shall very soon be in the Republic where all men are really equals and the only masters are the worms. My reason for requesting you to come was to speak of your unfortunate experiences—of a certain unfortunate experience in particular. You referred in your lecture to the execution of one called "Victor Lesueur". He died game, hein?'

'As plucky a soul as I ever dispatched!' said Robichon, savouring the burgundy.

'Ah! Not a tremor? He strode to the guillotine like a man?'

'Like a hero!' said Robichon, who knew nothing about him.

'That was fine,' said the marquis; 'that was as it should be! You have never known a prisoner to die more bravely?' There was a note of pride in his voice that was unmistakable.

'I shall always recall his courage with respect,' declared Robichon, mystified.

'Did you respect it at the time?'

'Pardon, monsieur le marquis?'

'I inquire if you respected it at the time; did you spare him all needless suffering?'

'There is no suffering,' said Robichon. 'So swift is the knife that——'

The host made a gesture of impatience. 'I refer to mental suffering. Cannot you realize the emotions of an innocent man condemned to a shameful death?'

'Innocent! As for that, they all say that they are innocent.'

'I do not doubt it. Victor, however, spoke the truth. I know it. He was my son.'

'Your son?' faltered Robichon, aghast.

'My only son—the only soul I loved on earth. Yes; he was innocent, Monsieur Roux. And it was you who butchered him—he died by your hands.'

'I—I was but the instrument of the law,' stammered Robichon. 'I was not responsible for his fate, myself.'

'You have given a masterly lecture, Monsieur Roux,' said the marquis musingly; 'I find myself in agreement with all that you said in it—"you are his murderer". I hope the wine is to your taste, Monsieur Roux? Do not spare it!'

'The wine?' gasped the actor. He started to his feet, trembling—he understood.

'It is poisoned,' said the old man calmly. 'In an hour you will be dead.'

'Great Heavens!' moaned Robichon. Already he was conscious of a strange sensation—his blood was chilled, his limbs were weighted, there were shadows before his eyes.

'Ah, I have no fear of you!' continued the other; 'I am feeble, I could not defend myself; but your violence would avail you nothing. Fight, or faint, as you please—you are doomed.'

For some seconds they stared at each other dumbly—the actor paralysed by terror, the host wearing the smile of a lunatic. And then the 'lunatic' slowly peeled court-plaster from his teeth, and removed features, and lifted a wig.

And when the whole story was published, a delighted Paris awarded the palm to Quinquart without a dissentient voice, for while Robichon had duped an audience, Quinquart had duped Robichon himself.

Robichon bought the silver candlesticks, which had been hired for the occasion, and he presented them to Quinquart and Suzanne on their wedding-day.

NAOMI MITCHISON

The Hostages

THERE were only three of us left now; the others had been hung over the ramparts, one every morning. Elxsente was still sick and we didn't know what to do with him; he was only a child, and cried for his mother at nights; some of the others had done that, and I would have too, but I was fifteen and had to set a good example. They used to take us out on to the walls, and whip us where the men from our own cities could see us; of course they had the right to do it, but some of us weren't very old, and used to cry even at the thought of it, which was bad for every one. But we could look out when we were taken up, and there was our camp, spread and shining below us; once there was an attack while we were there and we all cheered, but the Romans paid us back in kicks for that. I saw the banner of Mireto from time to time, and thought I could make out my father at the head of the spearmen, and my big brother with him; and once I saw a herald whom I knew, and called out to him, but he didn't hear me. Every day we hoped the town would fall, though we should very likely have been killed before any one could get to us; still, it was a chance, and better than being dragged out and choked like dogs at the end of a rope. We knew our people were pressing hard and might soon starve the town out; for the last week they had given us nothing but water and a very little bread; the one who was chosen to be hung every morning used to leave his share of the bread to any one he liked. There wasn't too much water, either;

the last day Teffre and I had given it all to Elxsente; we thought we should be able to eat his bread—he wouldn't touch it—but we were too thirsty.

I was awake all that night, though Teffre slept for a little. I leant up against the wall at the back, with Elxsente's head on my shoulder; he seemed easier that way. I thought about home, and tried to imagine I was in my own room; I wondered if they were looking after my pony properly, and I tried to remember whether I'd mended the bridle before I was sent away as a hostage to the Romans; I couldn't be sure, and it worried me.

When it was just light Teffre woke up and said he heard shouting; we both listened and I heard it too. He went over to the slit, but of course he could see nothing; he used always to think he might see something some time. But certainly there was cheering, and Teffre said he was sure we'd taken the town; but it wasn't the first time he'd thought that, and I wasn't hopeful, particularly as nothing else happened for hours. My back was very sore from the beating, and we'd had no chance of a wash for weeks. Elxsente was better after his sleep, and thirsty, but the water was all gone.

Then the door opened, and the man we called the Boar—we all hated him—came in. I wondered which of us he was going to take, and rather hoped it would be Teffre, because I was much better at looking after Elxsente—I didn't want it to be *him* anyhow. Teffre asked him what had happened—he never could learn not to—and the man hit his hand with the iron key, and then said, 'The General's come, and your people have all run away.' That was hard hearing for us; we knew it wasn't true about our army having run, but we supposed they'd withdrawn, and we were very unhappy, but we said nothing and waited. He went on: 'You dogs, you ought to be hung, but the General's begged your lives and you've been given to him.'

We didn't quite understand at once, and then a great tall man came in, all in armour, with a golden helmet plumed with a black horse-tail; he could only stand upright in the middle of the arch; he looked at us and asked, 'Are these all that are left?' The Boar stood at attention as he said, 'Yes, sir,' and then to us: 'Down on your knees before your master!' I don't remember what Teffre did, but I simply sat and stared at the General; one can't think very quickly after one hasn't slept all night. The Boar came over and hit me and I was afraid he was going to hit Elxsente; so I knelt, and Elxsente knelt, leaning against me, and Teffre knelt in the other corner. The light came in through the doorway, behind the General, and he looked very big, as if he could tread us into the ground; a little wind came in too and I heard the horse-hairs rustling against the bronze.

He was speaking to us, but I didn't hear it all; I was thinking that we were going to live, and I was glad and thankful, and then I thought that our army was beaten, and perhaps my father and brother were killed; I felt that I loved Mireto, my city, terribly, and that it would be awful if the Romans were to take her; and then I thought it might be better to die after all. I heard the General saying that our lives were forfeit, but that he had asked that we should be spared, and then about how wicked it was of the League of the Cities to have broken the treaty; I was wondering if it was any use my telling him that bad treaties ought to be broken, but just then Elxsente slipped forward and I had to catch him; he felt very hot and was breathing fast. The General came up to us and stooped over him; Elxsente threw his arms round my neck and held on tight with his face pressed into my shoulder; the General said, 'Don't be frightened,' and lifted his head quite gently; he asked how long he'd been like this, and I told him ten days, and said could we have some water for him. He asked if we had not had any, and I said yes, but that Elxsente had had his share and our share too, but he was all burnt up and always wanted more. He turned round to the Boar and the metal plates on his kilt swung against my face; he told him to get us water, and then felt Elxsente's head and hands, and told me he thought he would live. When the water came Elxsente let go of me with one hand and drank and looked up at the General, and Teffre drank, and then I drank; I've never tasted anything as good as that water; I felt quite different at once, and I would have spoken to the General to justify our cities, only he went out.

That day we had dried figs with our bread, and in the evening they brought some milk for Elxsente. We heard how the General had marched up secretly and surprised and scattered our camp and relieved the town; a few days afterwards the Boar told us peace had been made; some of the cities were given up to Rome, and the walls of Mireto had to be pulled down. Teffre and I talked it over; we wondered whether we ought to outlive the disgrace—*his* city was to pay tribute and have Rome for overlord—but finally we made up our minds to go on living for a little longer at least; we didn't quite know how to kill ourselves, and besides there was Elxsente; his city had to pay tribute too, but he didn't understand the shame of it, like we did.

By the time they let us out, Elxsente was much better,

but we were none of us very strong. They tied us into a wagon; we sat on the bottom, out of the sun, and saw the tops of the trees that we passed under along the road, but not much else. The journey took three days, and then we stopped outside the walls of Rome. There was dust all over everything, dust in our hair and ears and eyelashes, dust caked on our hands and feet, white dust on the bread and fruit we ate. The wagon was drawn up on the inside of a square, and we sat on the edge trying to see what was happening; prisoners—our own men—were brought in under guard, formed up, and chained; of course we all looked hard to see if there was any one we knew among them; often we thought we saw faces of friends, but they never were. Then one of my father's men was marched past and I shouted to him; he turned and called to me that my father had escaped, but he didn't know about my brother; still, that was something. There were women prisoners too, from the towns that had been taken, and armour and horses and gold cups from the altars of the Gods. Teffre saw one cartload from his own city and raged at being so helpless. And then Elxsente cried out and said he saw his cousin among the women, a white-faced girl with eyes swollen from tears and dust; we all called, but she didn't hear or heed, and Elxsente was terribly disappointed.

Then we were taken out of the wagon over to a heap of chains and one of the soldiers found light ones for us. Then we waited at the edge of the road till our turn came. The Roman soldiers went by first, crowned and singing; after them our prisoners, chained together; and more Romans; and trophies of swords and spears, and the pick of the cattle that had been taken; and more Romans; and a great line of women and children, and pictures of the battles, and ox-carts full of gold and silver, well guarded; and more Romans still, and more prisoners; and we were bitterly angry and sad. Then there was a place for us, and we joined the march with Roman soldiers in front of us and at each side. At first there was nothing but choking dust, until we got to the suburbs, where the streets had been watered, which kept the dust down and was pleasant to the feet. But then the crowds began, crowds of shouting enemies at the two edges of the road; they frightened me more than anything; we were so helpless and alone in the middle of them, and sometimes the noise would suddenly swell up into a roar all round us, and Elxsente would shrink up close to me; once or twice they threw things at us, but nothing sharp enough to cut. A man who walked in front of us kept on repeating in a shout that we were the hostages from the cities who were spared by order of the General and that the rest were hung. He said it over and over again like a corncrake: I would have given a lot to kill that man. We must have had seven or eight miles to walk in the sun at the pace of the slowest oxen; at first I looked about me and whispered to the others from time to time and sang our marching song under my breath, but later I was too tired to do anything but stumble along with my head down. My hands were chained behind my back so that I couldn't even wipe the sweat off my forehead or the dust out of my eyes. About half-way Teffre cut his foot on a sharp stone and fell, but one of the guards picked him up and helped him along. I was miserable about Elxsente; he wasn't well yet and the sun was burning on our heads; he knew he must go through the day without whimpering for the honour of his city, and he did it well, but I could feel how much it was costing him and I could do nothing to help him; I was thankful when the soldier on his side said, 'I've a child of my own,' and took him on to his shoulder for part of the way. The day seemed endless, but suddenly we were halted in a great square place where some one was speaking from the top of a flight of steps. I saw the General a long way off, wearing a laurel wreath and a purple robe, but I was too tired to see much; all those great white buildings were swimming in the heat and there wasn't a breath of wind to blow away the smell, that seemed everywhere, of leather and onions, and the hot crowd.

When the Triumph was over and our chains were taken off, we were locked up in a little barred room, a prison of some sort, with straw on the flag-stones. We lay there, thankful for the dark and quiet, and slept like the dead all night. The first day a woman, who seemed too dazed to speak, brought us food; the second day another woman brought it; she was Elxsente's cousin. He rushed up to her with, 'Where's mother?' and she burst into tears and put her arms round him. She had seen his father dead of wounds and knew his mother and the baby sister were burned in a house with some other women who'd tried to escape from the soldiers. But she could hardly speak about it; something terrible must have happened to her too; and she mightn't stay with us. Elxsente cried all that day, and even while he slept he was sobbing and calling, 'Mother, mother'; I couldn't bear it, I put my hands over my ears so as not to hear, but I knew it was going on all the time and I couldn't sleep at all. Teffre was very much upset; he seemed to have thought that when it was all over he could go back to the old life, but this showed him that he couldn't;

perhaps it was lucky for him that his mother was dead years before. Mireto had not been sacked, so my mother and sisters should have been safe, and I knew my father had escaped, but my brother might be killed or anything; and besides, I was the oldest and I realized it all better: how this was the end of the League of the Cities, our Gods were powerless, and our hope and honour in ashes.

The next morning we were taken away again; we were used to obeying orders now. An old soldier with a black beard was in charge of us; he wouldn't answer questions or let us talk among ourselves much. As we went through the streets a woman recognized us and threw a dead rat: it hit Elxsente; but I was glad it wasn't a brick. We had a long way to walk (though we got a lift for a few miles on a wagon that was leaving the town empty), first along one of the big main ways that went out between gardened houses and under arches, right into the country, and then along a lane with deep ruts, beside vineyards and cornfields; it was past noon when we came to a long low house with a walled garden where there were pomegranate trees. There was no one to be seen, and the soldier stopped, sat down on the bottom step of the ones that led up to the house door, and ate bread and onions. We sat on the ground beside him and waited, and the afternoon got hotter and hotter; we were all very tired. We'd had nothing to eat since early that morning—we hoped the soldier would give us something, but he didn't, and of course we couldn't ask. Teffre was complaining of his foot, which was badly swollen: I tied it up with fresh grass and a strip torn from my own tunic. Elxsente was crying all the time, quite hopelessly; his face was streaked with dirt and tears, and his hair was tangled into grey knots all over his head. I was unhappy enough myself; I tried to tell them stories, but that reminded us of home and made it all worse. Elxsente put his head down on my knee, and I felt his hot little face, wet against my skin. Teffre cried every time he moved his foot, and I was near it myself, but I thought of our being among the enemy and that we must show we were men. Still nobody came; sometimes we heard a cock crowing behind the house, and once a reaper passed through the trees in front of us with a sickle under his arm, but he never looked our way.

Then we heard voices inside the house and a lady came out on to the steps, with a maid carrying a basket behind her. The soldier saluted and spoke to her; she was all in blue, with the western sun on her face and hair. She ran down the steps and saw us. 'Oh,' she said, 'oh—you children! You poor children!' and in a moment she was beside me and had gathered Elxsente up into her arms; he lay there limp with his eyes half-shut, still crying. 'Have you been here all day,' she asked, 'with nothing to eat?' I nodded and she called up to the maid to bring food and drink quickly. I was glad to see how angry she was with the soldier; she sent him away and sat down on the steps with Elxsente on her knee, sobbing a little less. The maid brought milk and barley cakes and pears and grapes; we ate everything, and she fed Elxsente herself. Then the General came round from the other side of the garden; I knew him at once, though he was wearing a woollen tunic and sandals instead of armour; the bailiff (though we didn't know who he was till afterwards) was at his side. I stood up, and his wife stood up holding Elxsente to her breast.

He looked at us kindly enough and told the bailiff to

take Teffre and me down to the pool to wash. We went with him, Teffre limping badly; it was a broad, shallow, stone basin, with sunflowers growing round it. We stripped and went in and washed off layers and layers of dust and sweat, and swam among the lily-pads till he told us to come out. They brought us clean clothes and we put them on with our hair dripping; he took us back to the house, to a clean, light room with blankets spread on the floor for us, and Teffre sat on a table while some one bandaged his foot properly. Then Elxsente came in and told us how the women of the house had washed him and dressed him and been kind to him, and he lay down on the blankets and I covered him, and he went to sleep almost at once. Then the General sent for me; he was sitting alone in a tall chair, with candles behind him. He asked me if I thought we should be ransomed; I said I believed Teffre and I would be, but that Elxsente's father and mother were killed, so I couldn't tell about him. He sent me away, and the mistress met me in the hall and asked if Elxsente was asleep.

The next day we were left alone most of the time, to eat and rest, but after that, when Teffre's foot was better, we were given work to do about the farm and garden, under the bailiff; it wasn't hard—getting in the grapes and apples, feeding the geese, driving the cows home, and so on. Elxsente got well wonderfully quickly, and forgot about his mother for hours together; the mistress petted him a lot and the General spoke to him whenever he saw him.

But the weeks went on and the autumn was going; there were frosts at night; once round the pond and out was as far as we cared to swim. But none of us heard anything from our homes. And then one day the General sent for Teffre to tell him he'd been ransomed, and his uncle was waiting to take him away. In an hour he'd said good-bye to us and was gone; I've never seen him since. Of course Elxsente and I were glad for his sake, but it made me wonder what was going to happen to me; I thought of all sorts of things; perhaps the soldier might have been wrong about my father; perhaps he was dead and my brother was dead, and all our money was gone; perhaps I should never see Mireto and my mother and our house again. Every one was good to us, but of course we were no more free than any of the slaves, and I didn't like to think of all my life being like that. At one time I thought of running away, but I should probably have been caught, and anyhow I should have had to leave Elxsente; I had a plan that my father should ransom him too and he should come back and live with us and be my little brother, now that he had no one of his own kin left. We used to talk about that in the evenings.

But it was winter now. We were busy pruning the vines and fruit trees; Elxsente worked with me, but of course I had longer hours and did more. After it was dark the mistress used often to have us in and we sat with them, making withy plaits, while the General talked about farming and wild beasts and told us all his adventures. Sometimes he talked about Rome, things she had done in the past, things he said she would do in the future. I thought about Mireto and said nothing, but Elxsente seemed to believe it. We worshipped with them too: the country Gods are the same all the world over. Sometimes we went out after wolves and once I was in the thick of it, when either a hound or the wolf bit me in the arm. Looking back on it all now it seems such a waste of time that I didn't really enjoy it; but then I didn't know what had happened at home.

One day I was coming up to the house with my pruning knife and a great bundle of prunings to burn; Elxsente had gone in, but I had stayed to finish the row, and it was nearly dark; I heard hoofs behind me, turned, and there was my father! I threw down the bundle and ran to him, and he was off his horse and had me in his arms, all in a moment. The horse grazed by the road-side and we talked. Of course I asked first about mother and every one. 'My little son,' he said, 'you didn't hear all this long time! All's well at home, but you know I'd spent all the money we had in arming my men. There was nothing left, and I had all I could do to raise enough to buy you both back. Did you know your brother was taken prisoner during the siege? I couldn't find him for months; he had been sold as a slave in the Roman market, and I bought him back first: he was having a bad time. But I thought you would be well treated here—they've not been unkind to you, son?' He looked at the bundle of wood, and then at the bound place on my arm where I'd had the wolf-bite. I told him they'd all been kind and what sort of life it was; he put me up on his horse—it was fine to be in the saddle again—with the prunings behind, and we went up to the house. The General met my father and took him in, and I led the horse round to the stables and bedded him down.

When I came in they'd settled my ransom, and father said we should go home the next day. I was so happy I could hardly think, and then, with a jump, I remembered Elxsente. 'Oh, father,' I said, 'can't you buy back my friend too? He's got no one left, and I told him I'd take him home with me.' Father looked miserable and said he couldn't—I found out afterwards how hard the ransom money had been to come by—but that he'd try to later, for the honour of the cities. But the General said, 'I don't want to have Elxsente ransomed; I've another plan for him; call him and we'll see.' He came in, and the mistress with him; he ran over to me and took my hands: 'Oh, you're going,' he said, 'you're going back to your mother and I shall be left all alone!' But the General leaned forward, saying, 'Elxsente, you know I've no children of my own. Will you come and live with me always, and be my son?' and the mistress spoke softly to him: 'Stay with us, dear.' And Elxsente looked at them and looked at me and then looked down on the floor, wondering. And I said, 'Think of your City, Elxsente! Don't put yourself into the hands of the enemy!' and he said to me, 'Would it be very wrong to stay? I think I'd like to stay.' I would have spoken, but my father stopped me and spoke himself: 'You know that I'm of the Cities, child, on your side; so you can trust me; and I advise you to stay.' Then Elxsente went over to the mistress and put his arms round her neck, and she and the General kissed him, and called him son. And the General gave back the ransom money to my father and said to me that while there was peace I should always be welcome in his house.

The next day father and I set out for home. Elxsente came with us as far as the main road, and there we said our good-byes. Elxsente went back to the house, and father and I struck out over the hills for Mireto. We were back within the week and everything was right again. I found I hadn't mended my pony's bridle, but my brother had done it for me after he came home.

GEOFFREY MOSS

Defeat

THIS sister of Hasso von Koekritz has asked me to write this story.

My qualifications to do so are these. Twelve years ago, when he was assistant military attaché in Brussels, I knew him well. After that, it is true, I saw him only for a few days; still, he then discussed with me his position and its difficulties. Besides that, as I understood his mentality, I can interpret his motives, and can guess what his thoughts must have been. In any case, I was an eyewitness of what I am going to relate.

The race of Koekritz is an ancient one, and in the Middle Ages, when the Hohenzollerns were still unknown in those parts, and when Berlin was not yet even a village, this family with a few others dominated the Mark of Brandenburg. 'From Koekritz and Luderitz, from Krachten and from Itzenplitz, may the Good God deliver us.' This doggerel, dating from those times, gives a vivid enough suggestion of Hasso's ancestry. The lands of the family lay amidst those sandy wastes and endless reedy meres about the Spree, where, because of the extreme poverty of the soil, none but a hardy race could have lived at all, and where any adventure must have tempted. From the first they were fighters. A Koekritz served Carlos Quinto in Italy: one fought under Marlborough, several under Frederick the Great. A Koekritz fell at Austerlitz, another at Waterloo. The father of my friend led a charge at Gravelotte.

When I knew Hasso von Koekritz in Brussels he was

well off, and, to all appearances, more interested in sport, in social life, and in having a good time generally, than in the not too strenuous duties at his Legation. In the mornings we often rode together (for neither of us did work begin till the gentlemanly hour of eleven), and in the evenings we often dined *à deux* at Leymann's or at the Filet de Sole. Koekritz was fond of a good Bordeaux, I remember. 'A devilish good wine, I find this: a devilish good wine! Well! well!' and his long-sighted grey eyes would twinkle and his lean sailor-like face would twist into that tight, crooked smile which was so characteristic of him. He was barely thirty then, but of an uncommonly hard-bitten type.

One way and another I saw a lot of him. We went to the same dances: once we made a trip to Paris together: I mounted him for a few days' hunting in England: he gave me some duck-shooting at his home. I don't think that in those days I thought of him as being of any particular nationality. He was a jolly fellow to go about with: he spoke perfect English: we had tastes in common. Then came the war, and for ten years I heard nothing of him.

I

'If you are really determined on going there, I can give you an introduction,' said some one I met in Berlin. 'It's to a major in the Green Police, a Graf Koekritz.'

'Koekritz!' I answered. 'I knew a Graf Koekritz in Brussels once. Hasso his name was. But he was a soldier —in the Guard Hussars.'

It was the same, the man told me. An explanation followed.

After the war, the army being reduced to practically nothing, Koekritz, it appeared, had found himself a civilian. But soldiering had been his career, and his property had long been let to a farmer. The post-war rent, still the same and still paid in marks, brought him in yearly only the price of a single meal. He had, therefore, the alternative of living on his brother, who was head of the family, or of finding a way of keeping himself. So, when the Security Police had been raised, he had joined it.

'Look him up,' my informant in Berlin said to me. 'He'll be glad to see you. He isn't likely to find an industrial town on the Rhine too congenial. I'm afraid we Brandenburgers rather tend to look down on Rhine folk. They're a bit too modern, and a bit too soft to our way of thinking. You remember his *appartement* in the Boulevard du Régent? *Himmel!* He knew how to make himself comfortable. It must be rough on him now. Remember me to him, if you do see him.'

II

As soon as I had unpacked my boxes, I left the hotel and went in search of Koekritz. At the police barracks they gave me the address of his lodgings. Eventually I found the house, which was in a good part of the town. His rooms were at the top of it, on the fifth floor. There was, of course, no lift: and on account of my lameness I took some time to climb the stairs, and arrived breathless. I rang the bell and waited. Nothing happened, so I rang again. I was just going away when I heard some one moving about within the flat. Two women held a muffled discussion, some one lifted the shutter of the circular peep-hole which was matched by a medallion on the other half of the door, and peered at me through it. Then, rather distrustfully, one door was opened by a thin old lady. She wore a purple dress bound with black cloth; her grey hair was drawn rigidly back. She had high cheek-bones and sour lips.

'What do you want?' she asked uninvitingly, blinking at me, for the hall within was very dark, while the landing on which I stood was light.

'Can I see Graf Koekritz, please?'

She looked me over, her thin hands clasped each other. 'Come in.'

I did so, and she shut the door behind me, bolted, locked, and chained it. Then, without a word, she turned and shuffled away into the chill unventilated twilight, leaving me to follow her.

Pieces of large sepulchral furniture loomed around us. A confusion of stags' heads and Oriental swords crowded the dim walls. A joss-house lantern, surrounded by glass beads and baubles, hung so low that I almost touched it as I passed.

We went through a crowded drawing-room, thence through a dining-room, which had the air of never being used, but which had a table large enough for a dozen people. At the farther end of it were more double doors. The old lady tapped with thin knuckles.

'Come in,' said a voice.

I should have known it was Koekritz, even if I had expected some one else to be there. Indeed, I was surprised to find how unmistakably I recognized his voice after so long.

The old lady did not open the door, but continued rapping until it was opened from within. Then she slid away.

III

'Why! My dear fellow! My dear fellow! . . . what on earth . . .? Come in! come in!'

He took me by the arm, drew me into the room, and shut the door.

'You haven't changed a bit. Why, it must be . . . it must be twelve years. . . . But come along and sit down. This is nice!'

He led me, still by the elbow, towards the window. 'Which do you prefer—the rocking-chair or this?' I chose 'this', which had a castor missing.

What bit of good luck had brought me there? Why hadn't I let him know I was coming? He was obviously delighted to see me. 'Well! Well!' He looked me up and down, and his lips twisted into his tight, crooked smile. 'My dear fellow, this is nice!'

Though his voice was just the same as of old, his appearance had changed a good deal. He was very spare, almost angular. At the temples his brown hair was turning to grey. It was still brushed in the English way, and he wore it longer than is usual in Germany. The lines about his mouth were far more pronounced, and he looked more hard-bitten than ever. At the moment he was dressed in the faded grey-green of the Security Police.

'You came through it all right, then?' he asked.

I could still ride, I told him. We gave each other news of old friends. How was he getting on?

'Oh, not so bad,' he answered. 'Not so bad! I'm lucky to have a job. Lots of our officers have gone under altogether, you know.'

'Come for a walk. I've only just arrived, and I want to see the town,' I said.

The room chilled me. A comfortless-looking bed had been made up on a divan, and his brushes and toilet things were ranged along the top of a bookcase, but the room was one of those indeterminable chambers which large German flats possess. It might have been called a boudoir, but one felt that it had always been used as an ante-room to the kitchen; a place where a bicycle would be kept and polished, and where an informal evening meal would be eaten with the cook within convenient calling distance. It had been transformed into a bedroom with a minimum of trouble and forethought.

'Right,' he said. 'Wait! I'll change my togs. We wear plain clothes when we're off duty now—the army also. Democracy! It suits me, as a matter of fact. That was one thing I liked about the Brussels job. I never cared for hanging about in uniform all day. Have a cigarette?'

He shed his tunic on to the big central table. 'I'm going along to the bathroom. I wash there, you know. Messy having a basin and things here!'

I offered to come and watch him.

'I'd sooner—— Well—— It's better if you wait here. This *appartement* belongs to two old ladies. One of them let you in just now. Father was a General. They're pretty badly hit. No servant and that sort of thing. And the washing is done at home, and it gets dried in the bathroom.'

'Ash-tray!' He pushed one to my side, largely, I fancied, to avoid further explanations.

'Wait here, like a good chap, won't you? Shan't be a minute. Always a bit of a mess in the bathroom, you know,' he added, with confidential cheerfulness, as he went out.

When my cigarette was finished, I got up to help myself to another from the big dining-table, and having done so I took stock of the room.

The walls were covered with paper in which light brown, muddy green, and mauves predominated. The room was large, but there was only one window, the lower panes of which were of stained glass, depicting scenes from Æsop's Fables: the upper panes were frosted. This made the room even dingier. There was the divan that had been made into a bed, which was heaped high with some quilted *Bett decke*, and covered with a lace spread. Around another angle of the wall was a built-in cosy-corner, with family photographs let into the panels above. It would have held five or six, but could not be reached, because of a hammered brass table. There were some pictures, mostly engravings. One, I remember, was of Blücher, with a raised sword: another of some German philosopher or musician—I knew his face, but could not place him—standing bareheaded in a terrific thunderstorm. There was rather a nice old print of Sans Souci, with a dedication plate, showing that it had been given by Frederick himself. The glass-doored bookcase had been emptied, and served Koekritz for a chest of drawers and wardrobe. On the top of it were two or three old paper-covered novels. There was no bedroom furniture.

I had returned to my chair, and was just wondering how my friend amused himself in this place, when he came in again, rubbing the back of his thin neck with a towel.

'It's nice seeing you again, old man. You're not

married or anything?' he asked, as he struggled into a clean shirt. I reassured him.

He brought from the bookcase a blue serge jacket, and slipped it over the back of a chair. Its seams and elbows were rather shiny: I recognized the cut of it. On the central table lay the brass-bound trouser-press which I remembered.

'I'm really quite comfortable here,' he said, as if he had guessed my thoughts. 'They're quite decent old bodies, though not very cheerful. As there isn't a servant, one doesn't have to lock things up, which is a blessing. People aren't as honest here as they used to be before the war, you know. I suppose that's so everywhere. Really quite comfortable here, you know, and they get me some hot fodder, no matter what time I get back. And my job often keeps me pretty late. And even if they've gone to bed, there's a gas-stove in the kitchen. I've the use of the dining-room as well, if I need it. Besides, I don't know what the old things would do if I moved on. I don't fancy they've anything at all else left to live on now. Well! Well! I'm ready. . . . Come on! Where shall we go?'

We stole out through the dining-room, through the empty drawing-room, and the dark, chilly hall. Koekritz unlocked the door, and we went out.

'Cheer up! Cheer up!' he said, taking my elbow with a laugh which reminded me of the old Brussels days.

IV

The town proved a disappointment to me. The public buildings were in various styles of the last eighty years. None was interesting. Some had been requisitioned, and flew a tricolour. There were the usual wide boulevards with half-grown trees, the trams, prosperous villas in their gardens: clean, tall workmen's dwellings with red bed-quilts airing over the verandas and gay window-boxes: and all around the city stretched the usual model factories, by which it lived. In the ugly barracks there were French troops, and two reasonably smart sentries guarded the gate. A small detachment escorting a wagon passed us. No one took any notice of it, for this was in the old occupied territory, and there had been a French garrison in the town for more than four years.

'How do you get on with them?' I asked. 'Do they give a lot of trouble?'

'Oh! I . . . I've nothing to complain of. No army of occupation can be perfect. I expect, if it were our turn this time, we'd be just the same. A little friction here and there: nothing that amounts to much. Temperaments of the two races so different, you see. We're always carrying out everything to the very letter: we're unadaptable: we don't shrug our shoulders and make the best of things. Our burgomasters, and people like that, are always on their dignity. Even when we want to be pleasant, we're clumsy. And the French—you know what they are! They're always worrying about abstract ideas, *la gloire*, *l'honneur*, and always talking about being the victors; and looking for insults. But when one makes allowances for all that, things might be a lot worse. There are grievances, here and there, and some are pretty real. I come across most of them, unfortunately, because, when some one thinks he's been done down, he comes trotting round to us to complain. He might as well put his grievance in a bottle and float it down the Rhine in hopes the Dutch would open it, and get things put right for him. But when one thinks of what our occupation of their territory would mean, I don't suppose there's much to choose one way or another.'

We talked mostly of such matters, for in twelve years so much had happened to both of us, that most of the old points of our contact had been obliterated. There were so many subjects upon which I should not have cared to venture. I would not have been the first to speak of horses, one of his chief interests in the past. Obviously he could afford none now. Dancing—I doubted if there was any social life for him in this industrial town. The society of it even before the war must have been chiefly commercial, and the very real differences between the classes in Germany had always made the mixing of them difficult. When I thought of his old life in the Boulevard du Régent, I could not imagine how Koekritz now spent his leisure. So I kept as much as possible off personal matters, and our talk during those first hours together was largely of war and peace.

Inevitably we discussed the Treaties, and the like. Koekritz was temperate, with a detachment which somehow suggested to me that he had felt too deeply and too long about these things, and that he had kept his thoughts to himself till his bitterness had burnt itself away, and that there remained in its place an emptiness which it was not pleasant to contemplate. Perhaps all this was my fancy, for he spoke with his old dry cheerfulness. It was only sometimes, in a pause, while he skirted some subject, that this feeling came to me.

It was a mess! Of course, it was a mess! There it was! That was that! The war had lasted too long: too much had been destroyed: too many lives had been lost.

One couldn't have expected the people who came out on top to have been very moderate.

That night we dined together.

V

'You've been back in Brussels since the war?' Koekritz asked.

It was two nights later, and we were sitting over our dinner-table in the restaurant of my hotel.

I had been in Brussels for a few days. I gave him news of people we had known. We explored the past. What had happened to Miette? She had bought a little cabaret and was doing well, I told him.

'Miette! I can't fancy her in that role.' He smiled at me over his glass. 'But here's to her!'

He himself had been in Brussels during the war, but he had never stayed longer than he could help. There had been no social life. Most of his old Belgian friends had kept away from the capital. In any case, those had been difficult times. Did I know who had his *appartement* now?

'Good days those!' he said. 'Good days! Do you remember the night we raced old Villainquatorze's new Delauney back from Ostend? Or that fancy dress ball at the Monnaie? Good days! They'll never come again. Well! Well!'

Koekritz seemed very happy that evening. I had discovered some Bordeaux—really first-rate stuff. Even a *Flamand* cellar need not have been ashamed of it. I don't suppose he had tasted any for a long while. His twisted smile was less taut. No one watching him would have guessed that life was not still easy for him as it had been in the Boulevard du Régent.

His manner was just the same as it had been in those days. He still spoke excellent English, but the turning of his phrases gave a curious suggestion of being out of date. Then I realized what produced this impression. He was using the slang of twelve years before. That was all it was! His English had been anchored while the speech of the rest of us had flowed on. He was still saying the 'some wine', 'some night', which we had borrowed, but had long since discarded. And words I needed to express our changed conditions puzzled him. 'Axed' needed explanation: the ramifications of 'stunt' were not easy.

We talked of dead men and of past customs. England had changed, I told him.

'Not as this country has,' he said, with the slightest nod towards a table near us, where, as at most of the others, sat French officers.

Things had changed in Germany, fundamentally, and so quickly, too, he added. While he spoke, Koekritz watched one with his long-sighted grey eyes. Then sometimes he would look down at his hands and would turn his loose signet ring round and round, and smile to himself. And sitting there that evening, the recollection of these forgotten tricks came back to me. He was thinking of these changes.

'For example?' For a while he sat silent.

'Do you really care to hear, I wonder?'

He looked up suddenly. His glance was almost distrustful. I felt that we were approaching a subject seldom mentioned.

'Of course I do.'

'All right. . . . Well. . . . I dare say you won't understand when I do tell you! . . . Here the changes all came in a matter of days. They were obvious enough, God knows, but how we . . . say myself—felt about them you very likely won't understand. The thing that struck me most, and which, I suppose, I shall never forget——' He broke away from his subject and caught another. 'It's all over now, and there's a new generation growing up, and things will begin to improve soon—they must. . . . It's *some* wine, this you're giving me! A devilish good wine!'

'Go on! What was it?'

'All right! But it isn't worth hearing, I promise you: still, if you want to know, it was our arrival—what's the word? Oh, thank you—our home-coming. You see, when I'd ridden out with my squadron at my heels in new service dress, we'd passed the Emperor, as he took our salute, and we thought—I suppose every one did, both sides—that it was going to be a walk-over, just a few charges, and then in a month or two we'd be back, hung round with orders and putty medals. There were bands, of course, and flags and people shouting and Heaven knows what more of all that. I saw the look the Emperor gave us—he knew most of us personally, you see—and that was one of the remembrances we took away with us. Well, those four years went somehow. It was odd that feeling how the thing would drag on for ever. I suppose it was the same thing on both sides. But even till quite the end, though everything was—well—falling to bits, to us at the Front things were really still the same. We'd got a country. We'd got homes to go to. We'd been beaten before. A nation that does much scrapping must get a hiding sometimes. The French had been in Berlin before, but equally we'd been in Paris. My father was luckier. Six months' war and a victory.

Still, one can't grumble. I'd jogged my old charger through three enemy capitals in as many years, and I'm still on top of the turf! Well, to go on, we couldn't hold out much longer. The knowledge came slowly: it was bad watching the men. We were losing: we'd get bad peace terms, but it would be over.

'I hadn't seen the Emperor for the best part of a year, but my brother was with him at the end. Only two days before he said to my brother that, if things got worse, he could count on those who were by him to ride in with him and get finished. And then, after all—— Well! you guess what a knock what actually happened must have been! It was nearer to us in the Guards Corps, for we knew him, but for the whole nation it was much the same. We're a people that had been used to being ridden on a pretty tight rein: we were used to it, and we liked it. You see us to-day. No policy. Like a loose horse that's badly hit, and scared to death. That's this country! We'd staked such a lot on one selection! But people don't always run to what one thought was their form. Things don't always turn out as one expects. Do you remember the money I dropped on that cert. you gave me in Brussels?'

'Yes, go on!'

'You really want all this? All right! . . . Well, when we got back, I hadn't any squadron. We'd been broken up, and I came in leading a company of God knows what foot regiment. And the welcome we got! There was the President of the week-old Republic, all in black, looking like a Karl Strasse undertaker. Not a cheer! Well, perhaps half a dozen. None of the old black, white, and red we'd been fighting under: but a lot of half-starved boys waving their red flags. There were decent people, too, but naturally the men were old 'uns, and the women were mostly crying—always a bore! Some of the Bolsheviki people were for hooting us, but they hadn't the pluck. Not much of a meeting, was it? The worst part was thinking of the under-officers. There was nothing in front of them, you see; and they knew it. We were a glum lot, I don't mind telling you! For most of us it was just the end of everything. Odd the things that come into one's head sometimes, isn't it?'

Koekritz stopped.

'Yes?'

'Well, I've never troubled much over poetry, and that sort of stuff, but as we came to it and one saw the Brandenburger Torr rising up above one like a cliff, I thought of that bit about "All hope abandon". It was a dull day, and with those little red rags being fluttered about all round the foot of it, and the winter sky showing through its five arches, the Torr looked bigger and greyer than ever. God knows how many times I've ridden through it with my squadron, but I felt that day as if I'd never seen it before. We came level with it: the column wheeled round: it got bigger and bigger: and there we were, under the centre arch. Then the men's march sounded all loud and echoing—you know the way it does when troops go under a hollow place—and then I saw the little red flags fluttering under the bare trees all the way down the Linden, as far as the eye could see. It sounds silly, but coming through the Brandenburger Torr that day, one seemed to have left everything one had ever known behind one.'

Koekritz paused.

'Well, I'm a lucky fellow, and I've no business to have bored you with all this. I'm in clover, really. Quite an interesting job I've got. Come round one morning and look me up at the police barracks. You'll be interested to see my men. I don't suppose there is anything quite the same anywhere in the world. We keep them pretty fit—well fed—trained to the last ounce. They are mostly the younger under-officers of the old army. They've got sport and boxing. They're as hard as hell. They'll interest you.'

The manager of the hotel came to our table and whispered to me. 'It's nearly ten o'clock, sir. After that no one is allowed in the streets or in the public rooms in here: but if you and the gentleman with you would like to stay longer, I will speak to the French colonel. He is very amiable and usually makes exceptions for guests here.'

I asked Koekritz what he wanted to do.

'I'll be going back,' he said. 'I can't very well take favours in my position, even when I'm in plain clothes. There isn't very much give-and-take between us and the garrison just now. I'll stay a minute or two till the rest go, and then I'll follow suit.'

The waiter came, and I paid the bill. How long was I staying? Over Sunday, at any rate, I told him.

Koekritz played with his ring for a minute or two. 'I shouldn't, if I were you,' he said, looking up suddenly. 'There's something on here next Sunday and . . . well, there may be trouble.'

'Yes, I know.'

Our eyes met. Koekritz tapped a soft tattoo upon the table.

'Are you watching it for some one in particular?'

I let the reflected light flutter on the knife I held.

'All right,' said Koekritz. 'But it's only fair to warn you there may be hell to pay.'

VI

During the next two days I saw nothing of Koekritz. He was busy making ready for what might happen, he said, when we spoke over the telephone. Indeed, the preparations of both sides were visible enough. Notices were posted at every street corner, announcing that on Sunday a great demonstration would be held in favour of forming the Rhinelands and the Ruhr Gebeit into a republic under French protection, and to prevent the proclamations from being destroyed by the townspeople, armed sentries were mounted near many of them. The strength of the garrison was displayed in other ways: patrols of cavalry and infantry moved about the streets, and a detachment of light tanks took up their positions before the railway station and remained there for some hours. Examining posts were established at several important cross-roads in the city, and at these passports had to be shown and carts were searched. Indeed, traffic in the main streets was rendered almost impossible.

From the outside world we were completely cut off, for all the local newspapers were suspended, and either the postal service of the *Régie* trains had broken down, as usual, or mails were being deliberately held up. A military descent was made upon the Rathaus, and the money destined for the unemployed confiscated so that the number of 'discontents' should be increased. The burgomaster protested and was thrown into prison.

The townspeople on their side, profiting by the experience with Separatists in other places, were taking all manner of precautions. Barbed wire entanglements were erected by voluntary workers on Thursday, in front of the Town Hall, the post office, banks, and other public buildings, but had to be removed next morning by order of the French garrison. The shopkeepers could be seen overhauling their iron shutters, or barricading windows which had none. Front doors were boarded up and shored with timber. Everything of value disappeared from the shops.

The food queues grew longer, for the transport services became daily worse. The supplies of bread were exhausted before every one could be satisfied, and those unable to buy hung about the shops till dusk. On Friday the unemployed, for whom there was now no dole, made a demonstration and did some small damage in the town; but the police, attempting to disperse them, were driven from the streets by the military and were confined to barracks. Eventually some money was obtained and distributed, and thus order was restored.

VII

It was Saturday morning that I went to the barracks of the Security Police. Koekritz must have left word at the gate, for I was at once conducted through chilly stone-flagged corridors to the exercising ground behind the building. There I found him watching the training of his men. He nodded to me abstractedly and said nothing, so I remained near him in silence.

In various parts of the Square squads were being exercised in musketry drill, gymnastics, running, and boxing. Some were in shorts, some in shirt-sleeves, some in full marching order. The men were clean-shaven and seemed all much of an age—thirty, perhaps—and though they were hollow-cheeked and rather colourless, obviously they were extremely fit.

Koekritz stood very still, his feet apart, his hands clasped behind him. Whether he was intent upon the work going on around him, or whether his thoughts were elsewhere, I could not tell. His expression was not a happy one. His grey eyes did not move. He looked older, I thought.

'What do you make of 'em?' he asked suddenly, and without turning towards me. They were certainly in fine condition, I said. But there was about them something which made the Green Police different from any other body of men I had seen, but which it was difficult to define. One associates physical fitness with a certain stolidity, with perhaps even a phlegmatic bearing, but these men had a sort of uneasy alertness. One might have fancied that they had always to fend for themselves, lived outnumbered, and were ever on their guard. To watch them long produced uncomfortable suggestions. All this I tried to explain to Koekritz.

'I know what you mean,' he said. 'You see, they've been on active service, or something devilish like it, for nine years now. It's a longish time: and in the end it tells.'

Most of them had been under-officers in the war, he added. And short rations and the growing certainty of defeat had acted on them, both directly and also through the difficulty they had had in heartening their men.

'As a matter of fact, their job here is pretty heavy going, too!'

'Like yesterday?' I threw in.

'Let's talk of something pleasant,' said Koekritz as we moved off across the Square.

The boxing was earnest rather than skilful, but some locks and trips I saw being practised by another party were neatly done. The movements of the drilling squads were impressively, even jerkily, sudden, but too individual for parade smartness. One was conscious of personalities working together, where one would have expected, especially in that country, a machine. About the skirmishing there was a forcefulness which made practice very like stark reality. Few words of command were to be heard. In all that was done there was a grimness not easy to describe.

'You said something about the trouble the police had yesterday,' said Koekritz. 'Things like that are inevitable when you get a weak force trying to carry on the duties of its Government and another force, much stronger, doing its damnedest to upset it. And all that in the same town at the same time! I don't think the garrison here are much to blame. It can't be fun for them either. But anyhow, things like yesterday's show can't be helped, and my men realize it, thank God! They've had to do some pretty hard thinking in their time, you see, and they're not affected by checks the way younger troops would be. What's the worst for them is having to stand, as they do, between the French and the civil population. There are always—what's the word! Yes, thanks!—there are always pin-pricks. People get a grievance and they come to our fellows and hand in their protest. Then, because we can't do anything, they think we don't really care. It's that that touches the raw! I've felt it myself, so I know. Right on the raw!'

Did he have much to do with the inhabitants of the place? I asked; for I was in the town largely to discover their views. His work kept him in constant touch with the city authorities, he told me, but socially he had no more to do with them than he could help. It was not easy to fancy the Graf Koekritz of the old Brussels days without a social background, but I realized how utterly his life had changed. No, he didn't miss it, he said. For one thing he was too busy. But in any case, the more people he met outside his duties, the more people would come to him with grievances that he had no means of righting.

'I can give you an instance,' he said, as we watched some squads being formed up. 'No one's allowed to leave his house at night, as you know; well, there's a fellow who's got an *appartement* below where I live. His wife was expecting a child—the first. So off he goes to the occupation authorities and asks permission for the doctor to come that night, after some other place he'd got to be at. He couldn't get the permit. The rule was the rule and that was that! But the officer he saw couldn't leave it alone. "Haven't you Bosches got enough children as it is?" he says. They are always worrying about their own falling birth-rate, and I'm sure he only meant it as a joke. Well, it wouldn't have mattered, only the man's wife had a bad time and the child was born dead. That's how things happen. No one was particularly to blame. Still, every time I meet him on the stairs I've got to hear it all over again. What can I do? No one's particularly to blame, but the fellow thinks I could do something if I wanted to.'

The squads re-formed, the parade was dismissed, and the men trooped briskly but cheerlessly into the barracks, leaving Koekritz and myself alone in the empty Square.

'Well! Well!' he said. The hardness faded out of his eyes, the fixity of his lips relaxed into his twisted smile.

'They're a pretty good pack, aren't they?' he added, with a nod at the now empty doorways.

VIII

I had arranged with Koekritz that he should dine with me that night, but in the evening a telephone message was sent to say that he was too busy and could not come. So, resigned to a solitary meal, I was choosing my wine, when an English journalist, whom I had met in the hall, asked if he might share my table.

He had arrived by motor that afternoon, and had come to see what the Sunday demonstration would produce. We exchanged my local news for his of the world outside, for I had seen no paper for several days. Many thought, he said, that a *coup d'état* would be attempted in the town next day. The French, so his information went, were bringing some two thousand Separatists in their *Régie* trains from all parts of the Rhineland: their flying column, he called it. We discussed to what extent the movement was spontaneous, and I told him that the adherents in the town were said to number twenty to thirty.

Presently the manager stopped at our table and talked with us. He was, like so many of his profession, a devout internationalist. All this was a foolishness, he said. Times were bad enough. Look at the prices! We had been considering them—if from a different angle, we explained—but he passed quickly to another subject. These Separatists were mostly professional criminals, he said, and many were not Germans at all. This, in some cases at least, was true, I knew; for I had seen their dossiers and lists of convictions in the police barracks that morning. Why, he wanted to know, should the

French Army, which was now the chief support of his hotel, arm such people and import them into a town where no one was allowed weapons for their own defence? It would only mean more work for the French themselves. What was the sense in that! The Separatists wouldn't bring money to the town or his hotel. They'd either steal what they wanted or they'd pay in notes of their own manufacture. Of course, if the French did not prevent them, the Security Police would arrest them, armed or not, in the ordinary way. But the Garrison would never have that! And would we believe it, the procession was even to pass the doors of his hotel. He, at any rate, was going to take no chances. He was going to have every door barricaded and every window shuttered. So, if we wished to see the procession, we must do it from the balconies of our rooms. But why should it be allowed at all? It was all a foolishness!

'*Das ist nicht le business*, gentlemen!' was his polyglot complaint, as he bowed himself away.

The journalist and I discussed the chances of trouble. He had, since his arrival, paid a visit to the Rathaus and had heard much there. At a meeting of all parties it had been arranged that, as there was no way of preventing this influx of 'undesirables', every one else should remain at home: and, as the only protest which could be made, every street should be empty, every blind down.

Except the Communists, all had voted for this: and they, who were as opposed as the rest were to the Separatists, had only refused because on principle they never worked with other parties! They had ways of their own, they had proclaimed, to prevent their country from being broken up. It was in this possibility of conflict that the real danger lay, said the journalist as we sipped our coffee.

The restaurant, although it was Saturday, was almost empty that night. The blue uniform of the French showed vivid amongst the bare white table-cloths. There were scarcely any other guests. A sense of impending events hung in the air. There were times when no one was speaking and when the waiters, scurrying along with loose covered dishes, seemed strangely noisy. Once some one laughed and, surprised by his own voice, looked awkwardly about him. Once the lights flickered and went out, but only for a moment. The manager even forgot to ask us if we wished to remain after the prohibited hour: and not having noticed the time, we were surprised, when the Colonel rose as usual and walked down the restaurant pointing with his whip to the various tables. 'These can stay: and these! Outside, the rest!'

'The fat will be in the fire if the Communists really have a go at the other fellows,' said the journalist as we moved towards the door. 'The French are only waiting for an excuse to disarm the police. Then there'll be battle, murder—and the rest of it!'

On the first landing our ways parted, and, as I went along the deserted corridor to my room, the words of Koekritz came back to me with leaden insistence. 'There may be hell to pay. There may be hell to pay.'

IX

Soon after nine next morning I was on the balcony of my room: by ten o'clock the manager and a porter insisted on lowering the heavy roller shutters behind me: at half-past ten the Green Policeman on point duty before the hotel was withdrawn, and thereafter the wide Platz was utterly deserted.

Time passed, but the procession, which should have started its march at ten-thirty, did not appear. No one stirred in the streets: the stillness grew almost oppressive. For a while I watched some sparrows, and in doing so I let my cigarette burn out. Then, to my annoyance, I found that not only had I no matches, but also that the shutter behind me was so heavy that to raise it from outside was impossible.

Presently I heard on the still air the whistle of an engine. I concluded that one of the *Régie* special trains had arrived, but an hour went by and nothing happened. To kill time I had just begun to make sketches in my pocket-book, when in a side-street to the right of the Square a dog barked, and then all at once I heard the shuffle of disordered feet. Another delay. Presumably the head of the column had halted to let the rest of it catch up lost distance. Then the march was begun again: a few voices took up a weak-hearted song, and the procession hove into sight around the corner.

At the head two youths carried a double-poled banner. Behind them a large man in a belted trench-coat marched with a defiant demeanour, a heavy pistol in his hand. After him struggled the rest. Most were boys of, say, from sixteen to twenty-two, beardless, poorly dressed, with mufflers, or with their shirts open. The more dashing affected caps, the more abject, spiritless felt hats. I observed, besides, a few older men, mostly unshaved. There did not appear to be any particular formation, but five abreast was perhaps the average. Their song almost died out, was revived by some one in comparative authority, thrived for a little, and wilted again. No attempt was being made to keep step. Those in rear checked and then hurried uncomfortably.

Passing below the hotel, some of the procession noticed me with jocular remarks. The man in the trench-coat looked up, and our eyes met. He was of a swarthy, bull-necked, and dangerous type. He was an immense fellow, and I wondered if he were a man of whom the journalist had spoken. If he were, he had been a gun-man in Ireland, and afterwards a French secret agent and terrorist in the Upper Silesian plebiscite area, where he had been employed to prevent the population from voting.

I had intended to count the number of the Separatists, but I started too late, became confused, and fell back on mere estimation. When the tail of the column had passed, I did not think that there had been more than three hundred of them. I was wondering why so few had been brought, when a second body appeared from the same direction. This detachment was better organized, and indeed some sort of step was being kept. There was no singing, but two or three of the elder men called the pace in some dialect. This company wore boots of what I took to be the French Army pattern. Close behind it followed another, less disciplined but much larger. More banners, several little hand-carts, and a small rear party ended the procession.

These last files were just level with the hotel, when suddenly I heard shouts, some cheers, an increasing clamour, and then the rap-rap of revolver shots. I leant over the railings and looked down the main street into which the leading detachment had passed. The middle of the procession was swaying this way and that and was apparently being attacked from a side-street.

The threatened collision between the Separatists and the local Communists was, I imagined, taking place. Those who were still in the Square came to a standstill, looked anxiously about them and grasped their weapons. As far as I could tell, only a few of them had pistols. The remainder was armed with rusty and obsolete sabres or lengths of leaden gas piping. All had on their sleeves green, white, and red brassards.

Suddenly from almost below my balcony came a roar of cheers, and looking down I saw a mob of men breaking out from the concealment of a little alley. Some of them wore red badges, and one waved a red flag. These were evidently the Communists, who, profiting by their knowledge of the town, had made a feint against the head of the procession and were now taking it in rear. The surprise was complete, or complete enough to stampede the least disciplined of the Separatists, who broke ranks and scattered across the Square, pursued by their assailants. Sticks and stones flew in the air: some shots cracked out, but by whom they were fired it was impossible to tell. The two mobs, intermingling, drifted in confusion to the farther side of the Platz, leaving the space before the hotel strewn with missiles and caps, but otherwise clear. Then from my balcony the fight was hidden by the tree-tops.

In the street to the left, where the larger part of the procession still remained, a counter-attack was being prepared. The leaders formed up their men with unexpected promptitude, and small parties were dribbled one after another along the side of the Square and out of my sight. From behind the trees came more cheers and the report of an occasional shot. The fighting spread over the Square and groups drove each other backwards and forwards.

There was little shooting, and that was wild. Presumably no one had much ammunition. Which side was winning I could not tell. From the left the leading detachment of the procession was still ebbing spasmodically back into the Platz; while from the streets on the right the Communists were still being reinforced. Some of the combatants, badly hurt, were helped away by their comrades. One man I saw limping out of the battle to a tree, to which he clung for a while, till his grasp slackened, and he slid to the ground.

The energy of the fighters was waning, and both sides were drawing back, the Separatists to the left, and the Communists to the right, when from the farthest corner of the Square came cries, but this time of a new sort. Soon these became distinct:

Polizei! Grüne Polizei! Polizei! Polizei! Polizei! And all at once every one in sight began running towards the hotel. The mobs, again thoroughly mixed but still carrying on some sort of warfare, surged into the main street through which the procession had originally been moving; while some small parties vanished in other directions. At the exit from the Platz a few Separatists halted and started to fire at groups of police advancing under the trees. Then the tap-tap-tap-tap of machine pistols spluttered out. The Green Police had opened fire, but obviously they were aiming high, for bursts of plaster flaked from the upper stories of a house. The rear-guard of the Separatists waited for no more, and followed the rest in its retreat. Then from under the low trees men of the Green Police swept into the open, moving in diamond-shaped groups of four. Some of these parties followed the retreating mob to the left along the main street and, a little way down it, established themselves across the roadway. In the same manner all other approaches to the Platz were blocked. Some ambulance men arrived and took charge of the injured. Within five minutes order had been re-established.

Then for the first time I noticed Koekritz, scarcely distinguishable from his men, walking, pistol in hand, from one group to another. He passed by the hotel, visited the picquet blocking the main street to the left, and then returned to the Square. There he stopped and looked about him. From my balcony on the first floor he was only a few yards distant.

'Hullo!' I called to him.

He spun round quickly.

'It's you, is it?'

'It's over now?'

'I hope so. Farther down there,' he nodded towards the left, 'our next detachment has taken charge and is rounding the visitors into their hall. They can hold their blessed meeting and then, now we've got the streets clear, they can go back to their trains in comfort. They'll have earned their francs to-day! We've got the Communists on the trot. They're quite sensible really. And, now they've had their show, they'll go home.'

Had there been many casualties? He didn't know. Some of the injured must have been helped away. In his area there were two dead, one a local Communist, and the other 'some poor devil' not yet identified. Seven or eight others were badly hurt. There would be no more trouble, he thought, except perhaps from a few stray bands of Separatists who had turned to the right in the Square, instead of following the rest of the procession. These were loose somewhere in the town. All considered, it had gone off better than he'd expected; and that was that! And all he wanted was a smoke!

I waved a cigarette to him, but he refused. He couldn't smoke on duty.

'Will you dine with me to-night?' I called to him.

'Delighted! Thanks awfully! Same time?'

He looked younger, I thought, more like *Hasso le Beau* of Boulevard du Régent days. Anxieties had told on him during the past week, but now that the trouble was past, a little of his old jauntiness had returned.

When would he be off duty? That depended! The Separatists would have to be sheep-dogged?—No, of course not. Shepherded back to the station, and those of them who had not followed the rest would have to be rounded up and taken to their trains. His men would have to get their dinners, he'd have to visit the hospital to see about the injured, he'd have to write up his official report, perhaps he'd have to see the new burgomaster, and then he'd be free.

'Would eight-thirty suit you better than eight?' I asked. But before he could reply the attention of us both was drawn elsewhere. For from my right came a familiar rumble, and looking down the street I saw a French light tank rounding the corner into the Platz. It completed its turn, faced us, squared itself, and covered with its machine-gun the blocking picquet of Security Police through which it had forced its way.

'What's up now?' I called to Koekritz: and, as I did so, a troop of cavalry clattered out of the same side-street. It passed behind the tank: its sections wheeled in our direction and presented a solid front, as the slats of a Venetian blind do, when they are turned. Then in an unbroken line, stretching from kerb to kerb, they swept towards us. Alone in the middle of the empty roadway, Koekritz awaited them. I do not think he knew any more than I did what was about to happen. He faced their onrush, holding his pistol at his side. I thought for an instant they would ride him down, and I wondered if he would fire. But a few lengths short of him the leader of the troop shouted a command, and his men reined up suddenly. For a moment he and Koekritz regarded each other. Then Koekritz relaxed his pose.

'It's all right now,' he said, with at any rate an appearance of ease, and in excellent French.

'Order is established,' he went on. '*Messieurs les Separatists* are already in the hall which you have requisitioned for them. What do you want beyond that?'

They were only a few yards from me, and from my low balcony I could see and hear as well as if I had been watching a piece of acting from a stage box. This thought came to me, as I stood there, with my friend before me in I knew not what danger: and in this clash of reality with unreality I felt at once that irony which mocks us and will not let us be.

The leader of the troop did not answer Koekritz. Perhaps the expression of his face hardened. Behind him sat his men, impassable, silent, watching; and solitary before them stood Koekritz in his worn grey-green; a rather faded figure against the rich brown background of the horses, the chilling glitter of swords, and the riders' airy blue.

I had a feeling that more was to follow, that the troopers were waiting for something. Then suddenly I knew what that something was, for behind them I saw a thin stream of armed Separatists trickling round the corner, from the street by which the French themselves had come. In all there must have been eighteen or twenty of them. Once in the Platz they broke into three groups. One crept to a place behind the heels of the horses: another moved round the farther flank of the troop and took up a position opposite the hotel, and the remaining party was led along the pavement, past the fronts of the houses to a spot just below my balcony. Alone in the middle of the roadway stood Koekritz, now surrounded on three sides, the nearest of his men out of hail. All round him was the silence of suspense. He turned his head, and for a moment our eyes met: his lips twisted, but the smile failed: he nodded and looked away. I felt the French were about to humble him before those Separatists of theirs. It was not a thing I wished to watch. I retired to the window behind me and tried once more to lift the shutter, but I could not. I turned to the street again. Koekritz was still standing there, his hand on his hip, waiting. I had seen him in that attitude once before, years ago in Brussels. It had been at a *concours hippique*, and he had stood so, chatting, just before he mounted for his turn at the jumps. In a lightning flash of memory there came back to me the picture of that forgotten afternoon, of him in his scarlet and silver, beside his big roan. Then the throw-back faded under the present.

The leader of the troop moved forward a yard or two.

'Surrender your arms!' he called to Koekritz in a loud, clear voice.

Koekritz looked to right and to left where the Separatists waited, gripping their lengths of leaden pipe.

'I am on duty here. My men have restored order. If we are disarmed, do I understand that you will then accept the responsibility of . . . of keeping order?'

The leader of the troop looked full into his face. I saw the man's elbows close to his side, the pull on his reins tighten.

'Surrender your arms, I tell you!'

Koekritz raised his pistol. He swayed a little and raised his chin.

'If you disarm my men, will you guarantee to protect them against these?'

The Frenchman bent a little towards him. I had no idea what was going to happen.

'We French do not interfere in purely German affairs.'

The words came low, spiteful, and distinct.

Koekritz stood rigid, his pistol raised. Whether it was covering the other I could not tell. Then he turned and, in that meeting of our eyes, I understood the full meaning of what lay before him. It was a fate he had always dreaded: he had discussed it with me: and I knew the alternatives that faced him. He could surrender and be thrown unarmed to the mercy of that mob: he could refuse and be shot down out of hand: he could sell his life as dear as he might. But if, under whatever provocation, he should fire upon troops of the French Occupation, his own country would pay.

The silence grew tenser. I knew what I must do. I gripped the railing before me and shouted to the leader of the troop. I have no idea what I said. For perhaps half a minute I continued shouting at him. I suppose every one turned towards me, but I saw only that one man. Then for a second I paused, and he looked away.

I had failed, and I realized that nothing could save Hasso Koekritz: that every one was helpless in that land where only vengeance ruled.

The leader of the troop leant back in his saddle.

'For the last time! Surrender your arms!'

I gripped the railing more tightly and waited.

'*Bien!*' said Koekritz suddenly, and changing his grip

upon it, he handed over his pistol, with an extreme restraint of gesture.

The leader of the troop turned a little and shouted a word of command. The line of horsemen reined back a few yards. On either side of the roadway the Separatists shifted this way and that. In the middle Hasso Koekritz waited for them. A gruff voice shouted a command, and from both sides the Separatists began a slow, disjointed advance. They crept forward with their lengths of piping raised, ready to strike. Some guarded themselves with a crooked arm. Foot by foot they slid forward over the asphalt and closed in on Koekritz.

They were almost within reach of him. Again I called to the French, and as I did so, I saw Koekritz spin round suddenly and throw himself furiously upon one of his assailants. The man went down. Koekritz got under the guard of a second and felled him. He was turning on another when the first blow fell. It struck him between his left elbow and shoulder. The broken arm dropped to his side. For a moment he checked. Another struck at him and reached his head. He wheeled round, his face gushing blood.

I looked over the railing and measured the drop, but my lameness held me where I stood. Perhaps I went on shouting: I do not know. Afterwards the journalist told me that a French trooper had tried to intervene, but had been ordered back. I saw the next blow bring Koekritz to his knees, but he struggled up and fought on. Some injured man roared in his pain: the clamour increased. The Separatists must have been hindered by their very numbers: they had no room to swing their weapons. One of them who had fallen and was trying to rise, protected Koekritz from that quarter. He turned and charged for a gap in the ring. For an instant I saw him clearly, bare-headed, desperate. Then a blow struck him squarely, and he went down. The attack closed in and hid him.

Presently the noise decreased: the rain of blows slackened and ceased. The circle widened. Some of the troopers who had now dismounted drew near and joined it. In the centre at their feet lay a limp form in a faded green jacket. For a moment they stood silent. Then the tension slackened, congratulations were exchanged, and the French and their agents shook hands over the body which they had vanquished.

I leant back against the wall and caught my breath. Koekritz was dead. There was nothing that I could do.

All at once, from the farther side of the Platz, came the sound of firing. Below my balcony a sharp command was shouted. The soldiers doubled to their horses and swung into their saddles: the sections wheeled to the right: the troop trotted off towards the new conflict: the Separatists in their gangs followed. Then, while the cavalry were still crossing the Square, the fight at the other end of it swung into my view. By a corner house I saw three grey-green figures battling against a mob. Another shot rang out: one of them fell: and suddenly the fight dissolved into a side-street. The French reached the same corner: they and their Separatists turned it and disappeared.

A wounded dog, yelping horribly, limped across the Square and out of sight. In the distance the sounds of fighting rose and fell. Presently all was still. Below me on the smeared and trodden asphalt lay Hasso von Koekritz, torn and broken, but at last beyond defeat.

FRANK O'CONNOR

The Majesty of the Law

OLD Dan Bride was breaking brosna for the fire when he heard a step up the path. He paused, a bundle of saplings on his knee.

Dan had looked after his mother while the spark of life was in her, and after her death no other woman had crossed the threshold. Signs on it, his house had that look. Almost everything in it he had made with his own hands in his own way. The seats of the chairs were only slices of log, rough and round and thick as the saw had left them, and with the rings still plainly visible through the grime and polish that coarse trouser-bottoms had in the course of long years imparted. Into these Dan had rammed stout knotted ash boughs which served alike for legs and back. The deal table, bought in a shop, was an inheritance from his mother, and a great pride and joy to him, though it rocked forward and back whenever he touched it. On the wall, unglazed and flyspotted, hung in mysterious isolation a Marcus Stone print and beside the door was a calendar representing a racehorse. Over the door hung a gun, old but good and in excellent condition, and before the fire was stretched an old setter who raised his head expectantly whenever Dan rose or even stirred.

He raised it now as the steps came nearer, and when Dan, laying down the bundle of saplings, cleaned his hands thoughtfully in the seat of his trousers, he gave a loud bark, but this expressed no more than a desire to display his own watchfulness. He was half human and knew that people thought he was old and past his prime.

A man's shadow fell across the oblong of dusty light thrown over the half-door before Dan looked round.

'Are you alone, Dan?' asked an apologetic voice.

'Oh, come in, come in, sergeant, come in and welcome,' exclaimed the old man, hurrying on rather uncertain feet to the door, which the tall policeman opened and pushed in. He stood there, half in sunlight, half in shadow, and seeing him so, you would have realized how dark was the interior of Dan's house. One side of his red face was turned so as to catch the light, and behind it an ash tree raised its boughs of airy green against the sky. Green fields, broken here and there by clumps of red-brown rock, flowed downhill, and beyond them, stretched all across the horizon was the sea, flooded and almost transparent with light. The sergeant's face was fat and fresh, the old man's face, emerging from the twilight of the kitchen, had the colour of wind and sun, while the features had been so shaped by the struggle with time and the elements that they might as easily have been found impressed upon the surface of a rock.

'Begor, Dan,' said the sergeant, ''tis younger you're getting.'

'Middling I am, sergeant, middling,' agreed the old man in a voice which seemed to accept the remark as a compliment of which politeness would not allow him to take too much advantage. 'No complaints.'

'Faix, and 'tis as well. No wan but a born idiot would believe them. And th' ould dog don't look a day older.'

The dog gave a low growl as though to show the sergeant that he would remember this unmannerly reference to his age, but indeed he growled every time he was mentioned, under the impression that people could have nothing but ill to say of him.

'And how's yourself, sergeant?'

'Well, now, like that in the story, Dan, neither on the pig's back or at the horse's tail. We have our own little worries, but, thanks be to God, we have our compensations.'

'And the wife and care?'

'Good, glory and praise be to God, good. They were away from me with a month, the lot of them, at the mother-in-law's place in Clare.'

'Ah, do you tell me so?'

'I had a fine, quiet time.'

The old man looked about him, and then retired to the near-by bedroom from which he emerged a moment later with an old shirt. With this he solemnly wiped the seat and back of the log-chair nearest the fire.

'Take your ease, now, take your ease. 'Tis tired you must be after the journey. How did you come?'

'Teigue Leary it was that gave me a lift. Wisha, now Dan, don't you be putting yourself about. I won't be stopping. I promised them I'd be back inside an hour.'

'What hurry is on you?' asked the old man. 'Look now, your foot was on the path when I rose from putting kindling on the fire.'

'Now! Now! You're not making tea for me.'

'I am not then, but for myself, and very bad I'll take it if you won't join me.'

'Dan, Dan, that I mightn't stir, but 'tisn't an hour since I had a cup at the barracks.'

'Ah, *Dhe*, whisht, now! Whisht, will you! I have something that'll put an appetite on you.'

The old man swung the heavy kettle on to the chain

over the open fire, and the dog sat up, shaking his ears with an expression of the deepest interest. The policeman unbuttoned his tunic, opened his belt, took a pipe and a plug of tobacco from his breast-pocket, and crossing his legs in easy posture, began to cut the tobacco slowly and carefully with his pocket-knife. The old man went to the dresser, and took down two handsomely decorated cups, the only cups he had, which, though chipped and handleless, were used at all only on very rare occasions: for himself, he preferred tea from a basin. Happening to glance into them, he noticed that they bore the trace of disuse and had collected a substantial share of the fine white dust which was constantly circulating within the little smoky cottage. Again he thought of the shirt, and, rolling up his sleeves with a stately gesture, he wiped them inside and out till they shone. Then he bent and opened the cupboard. Inside was a quart bottle of pale liquid, obviously untouched. He removed the cork and smelt the contents, pausing for a moment in the act as though to recollect where exactly he had noticed that particular smoky odour before. Then reassured, he rose and poured out with a liberal hand.

'Try that now, sergeant,' he said.

The sergeant, concealing whatever qualms he might have felt at the thought of imbibing illegal whiskey, looked carefully into the cup, sniffed, and glanced up at old Dan.

'It looks good,' he commented.

'It should be.'

'It tastes good, too,' he added.

'Ah, sha,' said Dan, clearly not wishing to praise his own hospitality in his own house, ''tis of no great excellence.'

'You're a good judge, I'd say,' said the sergeant without irony.

'Ever since things became what they are,' said Dan, carefully guarding himself from a too direct reference to the peculiarities of the law administered by his guest, 'liquor is not what it used to be.'

'I have heard that remark made before now,' said the sergeant thoughtfully. 'I have often heard it said by men of wide experience that liquor used to be better in the old days.'

'Liquor,' said the old man, 'is a thing that takes time. There was never a good job done in a hurry.'

''Tis an art in itself.'

'Just so.'

'And an art takes time.'

'And knowledge,' added Dan with emphasis. 'Every art has its secrets, and the secrets of distilling are being lost the way the old songs were lost. When I was a boy there wasn't a man in the barony but had a hundred songs in his head, but with people running here, there and everywhere, the songs were lost. . . . Ever since things became what they are,' he repeated on the same guarded note, 'there's so much running about the secrets are lost.'

'There must have been a power of them.'

'There was. Ask any man to-day that makes liquor do he know how to make it of heather.'

'And was it made of heather?' asked the policeman.

'It was.'

'Did you ever drink it yourself?'

'I did not; but I knew men that drank it. And a purer, sweeter, wholesomer drink never tickled a man's gullet. Babies they used to give it to and growing children.'

'Musha, Dan, I think sometimes 'twas a great mistake of the law to set its hand against it.'

Dan shook his head. His eyes answered for him, but it was not in nature that in his own house a man should criticize the occupation of his guest.

'Maybe so, maybe not,' he said in a non-committal tone.

'But sure, what else have the poor people?'

'Them that makes the laws have their own good reasons.'

'All the same, Dan, all the same, 'tis a hard law.'

The sergeant would not be outdone in generosity. Politeness required him not to yield to the old man's defence of his superiors and their mysterious ways.

'It is the secrets I would be sorry for,' said Dan, summing up. 'Men die, and men are born, and where one man drained another will plough, but a secret lost is lost for ever.'

'True,' said the sergeant mournfully. 'Lost for ever.'

Dan took the policeman's cup, rinsed it in a bucket of clear water beside the door, and cleaned it anew with the aid of the shirt. Then he placed it carefully at the sergeant's elbow. From the dresser he took a jug of milk and a blue bag containing sugar: this he followed up with a slab of country butter and—a sign that his visitor was not altogether unexpected—a round cake of home-made bread, fresh and uncut. The kettle sang and spat, and the dog, shaking his ears, barked at it angrily.

'Go 'way, you brute!' growled Dan, kicking him out of his way.

He made the tea and filled the two cups. The sergeant cut himself a large slice of bread and buttered it thickly.

'It is just like medicines,' said the old man, resuming

his theme with the imperturbability of age. 'Every secret there was is lost. And leave no one tell me a doctor is the measure of one that has secrets from old times.'

'How could he?' asked the sergeant with his mouth full.

'The proof of that was seen when there were doctors and wise people there together.'

'It wasn't to the doctors the people went, I'll engage.'

'It was not. And why?' . . . With a sweeping gesture the old man took in the whole world outside his cabin. 'Out there on the hillsides is the sure cure for every disease. Because it is written'—he tapped the table with his thumb—'it is written by the poets "*an galar 'san leigheas go bhfaghair le ceile*" ("wherever you find the disease you will find the cure"). But people walk up the hills and down the hills and all they see is flowers. Flowers! As if God Almighty—honour and praise to Him!—had nothing better to do with His time than be making ould flowers!'

'Things no doctor could cure the wise people cured.'

'Ah musha, 'tis I know it,' said Dan bitterly, ''tis I know it, not in my mind but in my own four bones.'

'Do you tell me the rheumatics do be at you always?'

'They do. . . . Ah, if you were living, Kitty O'Hara, or you, Nora Malley of the Glen, 'tisn't I would be dreading the mountain wind or the sea wind; 'tisn't I'd be creeping down with me misfortunate red ticket for the blue and pink and yellow dribble-drabble of their ignorant dispensary!'

'Why then, indeed,' said the sergeant with sudden determination, 'I'll get you a bottle for that.'

'Ah, there's no bottle ever made will cure me!'

'There is, there is. Don't talk now till you try it. My own mother's brother, it cured him when he was that bad he wanted the carpenter to cut the two legs off him with a hand-saw.'

'I'd give fifty pounds to be rid of it,' said Dan. 'I would and five hundred!'

The sergeant finished his tea in a gulp, blessed himself and struck a match which he then allowed to go out as he answered some question of the old man's. He did the same with a second and third, as though titillating his appetite with delay. At last he succeeded in getting it alight, and then the two men pulled round their chairs, placed their toes side by side in the ashes, and in deep puffs, lively bursts of conversation and long long silences, enjoyed their pipes.

'I hope I'm not keeping you,' said the sergeant, as though struck by the length of his visit.

'Erra, what keep?'

'Tell me if I am. The last thing I'd like to do is to waste a man's time.'

'Och, I'd ask nothing better than to have you here all night.'

'I like a little talk myself,' admitted the policeman.

And again they became lost in conversation. The light grew thick and coloured, and wheeling about the kitchen before it disappeared became tinged with gold; the kitchen itself sank into a cool greyness with cold light upon the cups and the basins and plates upon the dresser. From the ash tree a thrush began to sing. The open hearth gathered brightness till its light was a warm, even splash of crimson in the twilight.

Twilight was also descending without when the sergeant rose to go. He fastened his belt and tunic and carefully brushed his clothes. Then he put on his cap, tilted a little to side and back.

'Well,' he said, 'that was a great talk.'

'It's a pleasure,' said Dan, 'a real pleasure, that's what it is.'

'And I won't forget the bottle.'

'Heavy handling from God to you!'

'Good-bye now, Dan.'

'Good-bye and good luck.'

Dan did not offer to accompany the sergeant beyond the door. Then he sat down in his old place by the fire. He took out his pipe once more, blew through it thoughtfully, and just as he leaned forward for a twig to kindle it he heard steps returning to the house. It was the sergeant. He put his head a little way over the half-door.

'Oh, Dan,' he called softly.

'Ay, sergeant,' replied Dan, looking round, but with one hand still reaching for the twig. He could not see the sergeant's face, only hear his voice.

'I suppose you're not thinking of paying that little fine, Dan?'

There was a brief silence. Dan pulled out the lighted twig, rose slowly and shambled towards the door, stuffing it down into the almost empty bowl of the pipe. He leaned over the half-door, while the sergeant with hands in the pockets of his trousers gazed rather in the direction of the laneway, yet taking in a considerable portion of the sea-line.

'The way it is with me, sergeant,' replied Dan unemotionally, 'I am not.'

'I was thinking that, Dan. I was thinking you wouldn't.'

There was a long silence during which the voice of the thrush grew shriller and merrier. The sunken sun lit up islands of purple cloud moored high above the wind.

'In a way,' said the sergeant, 'that was what brought me.'

'I was just thinking so, sergeant, it struck me and you going out the door.'

'If 'twas only the money, I'm sure there's many would be glad to oblige you.'

'I know that, sergeant. No, 'tisn't the money so much as giving that fellow the satisfaction of paying. Because he angered me, sergeant.'

The sergeant made no comment upon this and another long silence ensued.

'They gave me the warrant,' he said at last in a tone which dissociated him from all connexion with the document.

'Ay, begod!' said Dan, without interest.

'So whenever 'twould be convenient to you——'

'Well, now you mention it,' said Dan, by way of throwing out a suggestion for debate, 'I could go with you now.'

'Oh, tut, tut!' protested the sergeant with a wave of his hand, dismissing the idea as the tone required.

'Or I could go to-morrow,' added Dan, warming up to the issue.

'Just as you like now,' replied the sergeant, scaling up his voice accordingly.

'But as a matter of fact,' said the old man emphatically, 'the day that would be most convenient to me would be Friday after dinner, seeing that I have some messages to do in town, and I wouldn't have me jaunt for nothing.'

'Friday will do grand,' said the sergeant with relief

that this delicate matter was now practically disposed of. 'You could just walk in yourself and tell them I told you.'

'I'd rather have yourself, if 'twould be no inconvenience, sergeant. As it is, I'd feel a bit shy.'

'You needn't then. There's a man from my own parish there, a warder; one Whelan. You could say you wanted him, and I'll guarantee when he knows you're a friend of mine he'll make you as comfortable as if you were at home by your own fire.'

'I'd like that fine,' said Dan with satisfaction.

'Well, good-bye again now, Dan. I'll have to hurry.'

'Wait now, wait, till I see you to the road!'

Together the two men strolled down the laneway while Dan explained how it was that he, a respectable old man, had had the grave misfortune to open the head of another old man in such a way as to necessitate his being removed to hospital, and why it was that he could not give the old man in question the satisfaction of paying in cash for an injury brought about through the victim's own unmannerly method of argument.

'You see, sergeant,' he said, 'the way it is, he's there now, and he's looking at us as sure as there's a glimmer of sight in his wake, wandering, wathery eyes, and nothing would give him more gratification than for me to pay. But I'll punish him. I'll lie on bare boards for him. I'll suffer for him, sergeant, till he won't be able to rise his head, nor any of his children after him, for the suffering he put on me.'

On the following Friday he made ready his donkey and butt and set out. On his way he collected a number of neighbours who wished to bid him farewell. At the top of the hill he stopped to send them back. An old man, sitting in the sunlight, hastily made his way within doors, and a moment later the door of his cottage was quietly closed.

Having shaken all his friends by the hand, Dan lashed the old donkey, shouted 'hup, there!' and set out alone along the road to prison.

'SAKI' (H. H. MUNRO)

The Background

'THAT woman's art-jargon tires me,' said Clovis to his journalist friend. 'She's so fond of talking of certain pictures as "growing on one", as though they were a sort of fungus.'

'That reminds me,' said the journalist, 'of the story of Henri Deplis. Have I ever told it you?'

Clovis shook his head.

'Henri Deplis was by birth a native of the Grand Duchy of Luxemburg. On maturer reflection he became a commercial traveller. His business activities frequently took him beyond the limits of the Grand Duchy, and he was stopping in a small town of Northern Italy when news reached him from home that a legacy from a distant and deceased relative had fallen to his share.

'It was not a large legacy, even from the modest standpoint of Henri Deplis, but it impelled him towards some seemingly harmless extravagances. In particular it led him to patronize local art as represented by the tattoo-needles of Signor Andreas Pincini. Signor Pincini was, perhaps, the most brilliant master of tattoo craft that Italy had ever known, but his circumstances were decidedly impoverished, and for the sum of six hundred francs he gladly undertook to cover his client's back, from the collar-bone down to the waist-line, with a glowing representation of the Fall of Icarus. The design, when finally developed, was a slight disappointment to Monsieur Deplis, who had suspected Icarus of being a fortress taken by Wallenstein in the Thirty Years' War, but he was more than satisfied with the execution of the work, which was acclaimed by all who had the privilege of seeing it as Pincini's masterpiece.

'It was his greatest effort, and his last. Without even waiting to be paid, the illustrious craftsman departed this life, and was buried under an ornate tombstone, whose winged cherubs would have afforded singularly little scope for the exercise of his favourite art. There remained, however, the widow Pincini, to whom the six hundred francs were due. And thereupon arose the great crisis in the life of Henri Deplis, traveller of commerce. The legacy, under the stress of numerous little calls on its substance, had dwindled to very insignificant proportions, and when a pressing wine bill and sundry other current accounts had been paid, there remained little more than 430 francs to offer to the widow. The lady was properly indignant, not wholly, as she volubly explained, on account of the suggested writing-off of 170 francs, but also at the attempt to depreciate the value of her late husband's acknowledged masterpiece. In a week's time Deplis was obliged to reduce his offer to 405 francs, which circumstance fanned the widow's indignation into a fury. She cancelled the sale of the work of art, and a few days later Deplis learned with a sense of consternation that she had presented it to the municipality of Bergamo, which had gratefully accepted it. He left the neighbourhood as unobtrusively as possible, and was genuinely relieved when his business commands took him to Rome, where he hoped his identity and that of the famous picture might be lost sight of.

'But he bore on his back the burden of the dead man's genius. On presenting himself one day in the steaming corridor of a vapour bath, he was at once hustled back into his clothes by the proprietor, who was a North Italian, and who emphatically refused to allow the celebrated Fall of Icarus to be publicly on view without the permission of the municipality of Bergamo. Public interest and official vigilance increased as the matter became more widely known, and Deplis was unable to take a simple dip in the sea or river on the hottest afternoon unless clothed up to the collar-bone in a substantial bathing garment. Later on the authorities of Bergamo conceived the idea that salt water might be injurious to the masterpiece, and a perpetual injunction was obtained which debarred the muchly harassed commercial traveller from sea bathing under any circumstances. Altogether, he was fervently thankful when his firm of employers found him a new range of activities in the neighbourhood of Bordeaux. His thankfulness, however, ceased abruptly at the Franco-Italian frontier. An imposing array of official force barred his departure, and he was sternly reminded of the stringent law which forbids the exportation of Italian works of art.

'A diplomatic parley ensued between the Luxemburgian and Italian Governments, and at one time the European situation became overcast with the possibilities of trouble. But the Italian Government stood firm; it declined to concern itself in the least with the fortunes or even the existence of Henri Deplis, commercial traveller, but was immovable in its decision that the Fall of Icarus (by the late Pincini, Andreas) at present the property of the municipality of Bergamo, should not leave the country.

'The excitement died down in time, but the unfortunate Deplis, who was of a constitutionally retiring disposition, found himself a few months later once more the storm-centre of a furious controversy. A certain German art expert, who had obtained from the municipality of Bergamo permission to inspect the famous masterpiece, declared it to be a spurious Pincini, probably the work of some pupil whom he had employed in his declining years. The evidence of Deplis on the subject was obviously worthless, as he had been under the influence of the customary narcotics during the long process of pricking in the design. The editor of an Italian art journal refuted the contentions of the German expert and undertook to prove that his private life did not conform to any modern standard of decency. The whole of Italy and Germany were drawn into the dispute, and the rest of Europe was soon involved in the quarrel. There were stormy scenes in the Spanish Parliament, and the University of Copenhagen bestowed a gold medal on the German expert (afterwards sending a commission to examine his proofs on the spot), while two Polish schoolboys in Paris committed suicide to show what *they* thought of the matter.

'Meanwhile, the unhappy human background fared no better than before, and it was not surprising that he drifted into the ranks of Italian anarchists. Four times at least he was escorted to the frontier as a dangerous and undesirable foreigner, but he was always brought back as the Fall of Icarus (attributed to Pincini, Andreas, early Twentieth Century). And then one day, at an anarchist congress at Genoa, a fellow-worker, in the heat of debate, broke a phial full of corrosive liquid over his back. The red shirt that he was wearing mitigated the effects, but the Icarus was ruined beyond recognition. His assailant was severely reprimanded for assaulting a fellow-anarchist and received seven years' imprisonment for defacing a national art treasure. As soon as he was able to leave the hospital Henri Deplis was put across the frontier as an undesirable alien.

'In the quieter streets of Paris, especially in the neighbourhood of the Ministry of Fine Arts, you may sometimes meet a depressed, anxious-looking man, who, if you pass him the time of day, will answer you with a slight Luxemburgian accent. He nurses the illusion that he is one of the lost arms of the Venus de Milo, and hopes that the French Government may be persuaded to buy him. On all other subjects I believe he is tolerably sane.'

DOROTHY SAYERS

The Dragon's Head

'UNCLE Peter!'

'Half a jiff, Gherkins. No, I don't think I'll take the Catullus, Mr. Ffolliott. After all, thirteen guineas is a bit steep without either the title or the last folio, what? But you might send me round the Vitruvius and the Satyricon when they come in; I'd like to have a look at them, anyhow. Well, old man, what is it?'

'Do come and look at these pictures, Uncle Peter. I'm sure it's an awfully old book.'

Lord Peter Wimsey sighed as he picked his way out of Mr. Ffolliott's dark back shop, strewn with the flotsam and jetsam of many libraries. An unexpected outbreak of measles at Mr. Bultridge's excellent preparatory school, coinciding with the absence of the Duke and Duchess of Denver on the Continent, had saddled his lordship with his ten-year-old nephew, Viscount St. George, more commonly known as Young Jerry, Jerrykins, or Pickled Gherkins. Lord Peter was not one of those born uncles who delight old nurses by their fascinating 'way with' children. He succeeded, however, in earning tolerance on honourable terms by treating the young with the same scrupulous politeness which he extended to their elders. He therefore prepared to receive Gherkins's discovery with respect, though a child's taste was not to be trusted, and the book might quite well be some horror of woolly mezzotints or an inferior modern reprint adorned with leprous electros. Nothing much better was really to be expected from the 'cheap shelf' exposed to the dust of the street.

'Uncle! there's such a funny man here, with a great long nose and ears and a tail and dogs' heads all over his body. *Monstrum hoc Cracoviæ*—that's a monster, isn't it? I should jolly well think it was. What's *Cracoviæ*, Uncle Peter?'

'Oh,' said Lord Peter, greatly relieved, 'the Cracow monster?' A portrait of that distressing infant certainly argued a respectable antiquity. 'Let's have a look. Quite right, it's a very old book—Munster's *Cosmographia Universalis*. I'm glad you know good stuff when you see it, Gherkins. What's the *Cosmographia* doing out here, Mr. Ffolliott, at five bob?'

'Well, my lord,' said the bookseller, who had followed his customers to the door, 'it's in a very bad state, you see; covers loose and nearly all the double-page maps missing. It came in a few weeks ago—dumped in with a collection we bought from a gentleman in Norfolk—you'll find his name in it—Dr. Conyers of Yelsall Manor. Of course, we might keep it and try to make up a complete copy when we get another example. But it's rather out of our line, as you know, classical authors being our speciality. So we just put it out to go for what it would fetch in the *status quo*, as you might say.'

'Oh, look!' broke in Gherkins. 'Here's a picture of a man being chopped up in little bits. What does it say about it?'

'I thought you could read Latin.'

'Well, but it's all full of sort of pothooks. What do they mean?'

'They're just contractions,' said Lord Peter patiently. ' "*Solent quoque hujus insulæ cultores*"—It is the custom of the dwellers in this island, when they see their parents stricken in years and of no further use, to take them down into the market-place and sell them to the cannibals, who kill them and eat them for food. This they do also with younger persons when they fall into any desperate sickness.'

'Ha, ha!' said Mr. Ffolliott. 'Rather sharp practice on the poor cannibals. They never got anything but tough old joints or diseased meat, eh?'

'The inhabitants seem to have had thoroughly advanced notions of business,' agreed his lordship.

The viscount was enthralled.

'I *do* like this book,' he said; 'could I buy it out of my pocket-money, please?'

'Another problem for uncles,' thought Lord Peter, rapidly ransacking his recollections of the *Cosmographia* to determine whether any of its illustrations were indelicate; for he knew the duchess to be strait-laced. On consideration, he could only remember one that was dubious, and there was a sporting chance that the duchess might fail to light upon it.

'Well,' he said judicially, 'in your place, Gherkins, I should be inclined to buy it. It's in a bad state, as Mr. Ffolliott has honourably told you—otherwise, of course, it would be exceedingly valuable; but, apart from the lost pages, it's a very nice clean copy, and certainly worth five shillings to you, if you think of starting a collection.'

Till that moment, the viscount had obviously been more impressed by the cannibals than by the state of the margins, but the idea of figuring next term at Mr. Bultridge's as a collector of rare editions had undeniable charm.

'None of the other fellows collect books,' he said;

'they collect stamps, mostly. I think stamps are rather ordinary, don't you, Uncle Peter? I was rather thinking of giving up stamps. Mr. Porter, who takes us for history, has got a lot of books like yours, and he is a splendid man at footer.'

Rightly interpreting this reference to Mr. Porter, Lord Peter gave it as his opinion that book-collecting could be a perfectly manly pursuit. Girls, he said, practically never took it up, because it meant so much learning about dates and type-faces and other technicalities which called for a masculine brain.

'Besides,' he added, 'it's a very interesting book in itself, you know. Well worth dipping into.'

'I'll take it, please,' said the viscount, blushing a little at transacting so important and expensive a piece of business; for the duchess did not encourage lavish spending by little boys, and was strict in the matter of allowances.

Mr. Ffolliott bowed, and took the *Cosmographia* away to wrap it up.

'Are you all right for cash?' inquired Lord Peter discreetly. 'Or can I be of temporary assistance?'

'No, thank you, uncle; I've got Aunt Mary's half-crown and four shillings of my pocket-money, because, you see, with the measles happening, we didn't have our dormitory spread, and I was saving up for that.'

The business being settled in this gentlemanly manner, and the budding bibliophile taking personal and immediate charge of the stout, square volume, a taxi was chartered which, in due course of traffic delays, brought the *Cosmographia* to 110A Piccadilly.

'And who, Bunter, is Mr. Wilberforce Pope?'

'I do not think we know the gentleman, my lord. He

is asking to see your lordship for a few minutes on business.'

'He probably wants me to find a lost dog for his maiden aunt. What it is to have acquired a reputation as a sleuth! Show him in. Gherkins, if this good gentleman's business turns out to be private, you'd better retire into the dining-room.'

'Yes, Uncle Peter,' said the viscount dutifully. He was extended on his stomach on the library hearthrug, laboriously picking his way through the more exciting-looking bits of the *Cosmographia*, with the aid of Messrs. Lewis & Short, whose monumental compilation he had hitherto looked upon as a barbarous invention for the annoyance of upper forms.

Mr. Wilberforce Pope turned out to be a rather plump, fair gentleman in the late thirties, with a prematurely bald forehead, horn-rimmed spectacles, and an engaging manner.

'You will excuse my intrusion, won't you?' he began. 'I'm sure you must think me a terrible nuisance. But I wormed your name and address out of Mr. Ffolliott. Not his fault, really. You won't blame him, will you? I positively badgered the poor man. Sat down on his doorstep and refused to go, though the boy was putting up the shutters. I'm afraid you will think me very silly when you know what it's all about. But you really mustn't hold poor Mr. Ffolliott responsible, now, will you?'

'Not at all,' said his lordship. 'I mean, I'm charmed and all that sort of thing. Something I can do for you about books? You're a collector, perhaps? Will you have a drink or anything?'

'Well, no,' said Mr. Pope, with a faint giggle. 'No, not

exactly a collector. Thank you very much, just a spot—no, no, literally a spot. Thank you; no'—he glanced round the bookshelves, with their rows of rich old leather bindings—'certainly not a collector. But I happen to be—er, interested—sentimentally interested—in a purchase you made yesterday. Really, such a very small matter. You will think it foolish. But I am told you are the present owner of a copy of Munster's *Cosmographia*, which used to belong to my uncle, Dr. Conyers.'

Gherkins looked up suddenly, seeing that the conversation had a personal interest for him.

'Well, that's not quite correct,' said Wimsey. 'I was there at the time, but the actual purchaser is my nephew. Gerald, Mr. Pope is interested in your *Cosmographia*. My nephew, Lord St. George.'

'How do you do, young man,' said Mr. Pope affably. 'I see that the collecting spirit runs in the family. A great Latin scholar, too, I expect, eh? Ready to decline *jusjurandum* with the best of us? Ha, ha! And what are you going to do when you grow up? Be Lord Chancellor, eh? Now, I bet you think you'd rather be an engine-driver, what, what?'

'No, thank you,' said the viscount, with aloofness.

'What, not an engine-driver? Well, now, I want you to be a real business man this time. Put through a book deal, you know. Your uncle will see I offer you a fair price, what? Ha, ha! Now, you see, that picture-book of yours has a great value for me that it wouldn't have for anybody else. When *I* was a little boy of your age it was one of my very greatest joys. I used to have it to look at on Sundays. Ah, dear! the happy hours I used to spend with those quaint old engravings, and the funny old maps with the ships and salamanders and "*Hic dracones*"—you know what *that* means, I dare say. What does it mean?'

'Here are dragons,' said the viscount, unwillingly but still politely.

'Quite right. I *knew* you were a scholar.'

'It's a very attractive book,' said Lord Peter. 'My nephew was quite entranced by the famous Cracow monster.'

'Ah yes—a glorious monster, isn't it?' agreed Mr. Pope, with enthusiasm. 'Many's the time I've fancied myself as Sir Lancelot or somebody on a white war horse, charging that monster, lance in rest, with the captive princess cheering me on. Ah! childhood! You're living the happiest days of your life, young man. You won't believe me, but you are.'

'Now what is it exactly you want my nephew to do?' inquired Lord Peter a little sharply.

'Quite right, quite right. Well now, you know, my uncle, Dr. Conyers, sold his library a few months ago. I was abroad at the time, and it was only yesterday, when I went down to Yelsall on a visit, that I learnt the dear old book had gone with the rest. I can't tell you how distressed I was. I know it's not valuable—a great many pages missing and all that—but I can't bear to think of its being gone. So, purely from sentimental reasons, as I said, I hurried off to Ffolliott's to see if I could get it back. I was quite upset to find I was too late, and gave poor Mr. Ffolliott no peace till he told me the name of the purchaser. Now, you see, Lord St. George, I'm here to make you an offer for the book. Come, now, double what you gave for it. That's a good offer, isn't it, Lord Peter? Ha, ha! And you will be doing me a very great kindness as well.'

Viscount St. George looked rather distressed, and turned appealingly to his uncle.

'Well, Gerald,' said Lord Peter, 'it's your affair, you know. What do you say?'

The viscount stood first on one leg and then on the other. The career of a book-collector evidently had its problems, like other careers.

'If you please, Uncle Peter,' he said, with embarrassment, 'may I whisper?'

'It's not usually considered the thing to whisper, Gherkins, but you could ask Mr. Pope for time to consider his offer. Or you could say you would prefer to consult me first. That would be quite in order.'

'Then, if you don't mind, Mr. Pope, I should like to consult my uncle first.'

'Certainly, certainly; ha, ha!' said Mr. Pope. 'Very prudent to consult a collector of greater experience, what? Ah! the younger generation, eh, Lord Peter? Regular little business men already.'

'Excuse us, then, for one moment,' said Lord Peter, and drew his nephew into the dining-room.

'I say, Uncle Peter,' said the collector breathlessly, when the door was shut, '*need* I give him my book? I don't think he's a very nice man. I *hate* people who ask you to decline nouns for them.'

'Certainly you needn't, Gherkins, if you don't want to. The book is yours, and you've a right to it.'

'What would *you* do, uncle?'

Before replying, Lord Peter, in the most surprising manner, tiptoed gently to the door which communicated with the library and flung it suddenly open, in time to catch Mr. Pope kneeling on the hearthrug intently turning over the pages of the coveted volume, which lay as the owner had left it. He started to his feet in a flurried manner as the door opened.

'Do help yourself, Mr. Pope, won't you?' cried Lord Peter hospitably, and closed the door again.

'What is it, Uncle Peter?'

'If you want my advice, Gherkins, I should be rather careful how you had any dealings with Mr. Pope. I don't think he's telling the truth. He called those woodcuts engravings—though, of course, that may be just his ignorance. But I can't believe that he spent all his childhood's Sunday afternoons studying those maps and picking out the dragons in them, because, as you may have noticed for yourself, old Munster put very few dragons into his maps. They're mostly just plain maps—a bit queer to our ideas of geography, but perfectly straightforward. That was why I brought in the Cracow monster, and, you see, he thought it was some sort of dragon.'

'Oh, I say, uncle! So you said that on purpose!'

'If Mr. Pope wants the *Cosmographia*, it's for some reason he doesn't want to tell us about. And, that being so, I wouldn't be in too big a hurry to sell, if the book were mine. See?'

'Do you mean there's something frightfully valuable about the book, which we don't know?'

'Possibly.'

'How exciting! It's just like a story in the *Boys' Friend Library*. What am I to say to him, uncle?'

'Well, in your place I wouldn't be dramatic or anything. I'd just say you've considered the matter, and you've taken a fancy to the book and have decided not to sell. You thank him for his offer, of course.'

'Yes—er, won't you say it for me, uncle?'

'I think it would look better if you did it yourself.'

'Yes, perhaps it would. Will he be very cross?'

'Possibly,' said Lord Peter, 'but, if he is, he won't let on. Ready?'

The consulting committee accordingly returned to the library. Mr. Pope had prudently retired from the hearthrug and was examining a distant bookcase.

'Thank you very much for your offer, Mr. Pope,' said the viscount, striding stoutly up to him, 'but I have considered it, and I have taken a—a—a fancy for the book and decided not to sell.'

'Sorry and all that,' put in Lord Peter, 'but my nephew's adamant about it. No, it isn't the price; he wants the book. Wish I could oblige you, but it isn't in my hands. Won't you take something else before you go? Really? Ring the bell, Gherkins. My man will see you to the lift. *Good* evening.'

When the visitor had gone, Lord Peter returned and thoughtfully picked up the book.

'We were awful idiots to leave him with it, Gherkins, even for a moment. Luckily, there's no harm done.'

'You don't think he found out anything while we were away, do you, uncle?' gasped Gherkins, open-eyed.

'I'm sure he didn't.'

'Why?'

'He offered me fifty pounds for it on the way to the door. Gave the game away. H'm! Bunter.'

'My lord?'

'Put this book in the safe and bring me back the keys.

And you'd better set all the burglar alarms when you lock up.'

'Oo—er!' said Viscount St. George.

On the third morning after the visit of Mr. Wilberforce Pope, the viscount was seated at a very late breakfast in his uncle's flat, after the most glorious and soul-satisfying night that ever boy experienced. He was almost too excited to eat the kidneys and bacon placed before him by Bunter, whose usual impeccable manner was not in the least impaired by a rapidly swelling and blackening eye.

It was about two in the morning that Gherkins—who had not slept very well, owing to too lavish and grown-up a dinner and theatre the evening before—became aware of a stealthy sound somewhere in the direction of the fire-escape. He had got out of bed and crept very softly into Lord Peter's room and woken him up. He had said: 'Uncle Peter, I'm sure there's burglars on the fire-escape.' And Uncle Peter, instead of saying, 'Nonsense, Gherkins, hurry up and get back to bed,' had sat up and listened and said: 'By Jove, Gherkins, I believe you're right.' And had sent Gherkins to call Bunter. And on his return, Gherkins, who had always regarded his uncle as a very top-hatted sort of person, actually saw him take from his handkerchief-drawer an undeniable automatic pistol.

It was at this point that Lord Peter was apotheosed from the state of Quite Decent Uncle to that of Glorified Uncle. He said:

'Look here, Gherkins, we don't know how many of these blighters there'll be, so you must be jolly smart and do anything I say sharp, on the word of command—even if I have to say "Scoot". Promise?'

Gherkins promised, with his heart thumping, and they sat waiting in the dark, till suddenly a little electric bell rang sharply just over the head of Lord Peter's bed and a green light shone out.

'The library window,' said his lordship, promptly silencing the bell by turning a switch. 'If they heard, they may think better of it. We'll give them a few minutes.'

They gave them five minutes, and then crept very quietly down the passage.

'Go round by the dining-room, Bunter,' said his lordship; 'they may bolt that way.'

With infinite precaution, he unlocked and opened the library door, and Gherkins noticed how silently the locks moved.

A circle of light from an electric torch was moving slowly along the bookshelves. The burglars had obviously heard nothing of the counter-attack. Indeed, they seemed to have troubles enough of their own to keep their attention occupied. As his eyes grew accustomed to the dim light, Gherkins made out that one man was standing holding the torch, while the other took down and examined the books. It was fascinating to watch his apparently disembodied hands move along the shelves in the torch-light.

The men muttered discontentedly. Obviously the job was proving a harder one than they had bargained for. The habit of ancient authors of abbreviating the titles on the backs of their volumes, or leaving them completely untitled, made things extremely awkward. From time to time the man with the torch extended his hand into the light. It held a piece of paper, which they anxiously compared with the title-page of a book. Then the volume was replaced and the tedious search went on.

Suddenly some slight noise—Gherkins was sure *he* did not make it; it may have been Bunter in the dining-room —seemed to catch the ear of the kneeling man.

'Wot's that?' he gasped, and his startled face swung round into view.

'Hands up!' said Lord Peter, and switched the light on.

The second man made one leap for the dining-room door, where a smash and an oath proclaimed that he had encountered Bunter. The kneeling man shot his hands up like a marionette.

'Gherkins,' said Lord Peter, 'do you think you can go across to that gentleman by the bookcase and relieve him of the article which is so inelegantly distending the right-hand pocket of his coat? Wait a minute. Don't on any account get between him and my pistol, and mind you take the thing out *very* carefully. There's no hurry. That's splendid. Just point it at the floor while you bring it across, would you? Thanks. Bunter has managed for himself, I see. Now run into my bedroom, and in the bottom of my wardrobe you will find a bundle of stout cord. Oh! I beg your pardon; yes, put your hands down by all means. It must be very tiring exercise.'

The arms of the intruders being secured behind their backs with a neatness which Gherkins felt to be worthy of the best traditions of Sexton Blake, Lord Peter motioned his captives to sit down and dispatched Bunter for whisky-and-soda.

'Before we send for the police,' said Lord Peter, 'you would do me a great personal favour by telling me what you were looking for, and who sent you. Ah! thanks, Bunter. As our guests are not at liberty to use their hands, perhaps you would be kind enough to assist them to a drink. Now then, say when.'

'Well, you're a gentleman, guv'nor,' said the First Burglar, wiping his mouth politely on his shoulder, the back of his hand not being available. 'If we'd a known wot a job this wos going' ter be, blow me if we'd a touched it. The bloke said, ses 'e, "It's takin' candy from a baby," 'e ses. "The gentleman's a reg'lar softie," 'e ses, "one o' these 'ere sersiety toffs wiv a maggot fer old books," that's wot 'e ses, "an' ef yer can find this 'ere old book fer me," 'e ses, "there's a pony for yer." Well! Sech a job! 'E didn't mention as 'ow there'd be five 'undred fousand bleedin' ole books all as alike as a regiment o' bleedin' dragoons. Nor as 'ow yer kept a nice little machine-gun like that 'andy by the bedside, *nor* yet as 'ow yer was so bleedin' good at tyin' knots in a bit o' string. No—'e didn't think ter mention them things.'

'Deuced unsporting of him,' said his lordship. 'Do you happen to know the gentleman's name?'

'No—that was another o' them things wot 'e didn't mention. 'E's a stout, fair party, wiv 'orn rims to 'is goggles and a bald 'ead. One o' these 'ere philanthropists, I reckon. A friend o' mine, wot got inter trouble onct, got work froo 'im, and the gentleman comes round and ses to 'im, 'e ses, "Could yer find me a couple o' lads ter do a little job?" 'e ses, an' my friend, finkin' no 'arm, you see, guv'nor, but wot it might be a bit of a joke like, 'e gets 'old of my pal an' me, an' we meets the gentleman in a pub dahn Whitechapel way. W'ich we was ter meet 'im there again Friday night, us 'avin' allowed that time fer ter git 'old of the book.'

'The book being, if I may hazard a guess, the *Cosmographia Universalis*?'

'Sumfink like that, guv'nor. I got its jaw-breakin' name wrote down on a bit o' paper, wot my pal 'ad in 'is 'and. Wot did yer do wiv that 'ere bit o' paper, Bill?'

'Well, look here,' said Lord Peter, 'I'm afraid I must send for the police, but I think it likely, if you give us your assistance to get hold of your gentleman, whose name I strongly suspect to be Wilberforce Pope, that you will get off pretty easily. Telephone the police, Bunter, and then go and put something on that eye of yours. Gherkins, we'll give these gentlemen another drink, and then I think perhaps you'd better hop back to bed; the fun's over. No? Well, put a good thick coat on, there's a good fellow, because what your mother will say to me if you catch a cold I don't like to think.'

So the police had come and taken the burglars away, and now Detective-Inspector Parker, of Scotland Yard, a great personal friend of Lord Peter's, sat toying with a cup of coffee and listening to the story.

'But what's the matter with the jolly old book, anyhow, to make it so popular?' he demanded.

'I don't know,' replied Wimsey, 'but after Mr. Pope's little visit the other day I got kind of intrigued about it and had a look through it. I've got a hunch it may turn out rather valuable, after all. Unsuspected beauties and all that sort of thing. If only Mr. Pope had been a trifle more accurate in his facts, he might have got away with something to which I feel pretty sure he isn't entitled. Anyway, when I'd seen—what I saw, I wrote off to Dr. Conyers of Yelsall Manor, the late owner——'

'Conyers, the cancer man?'

'Yes. He's done some pretty important research in his time, I fancy. Getting on now, though; about seventy-eight, I fancy. I hope he's more honest than his nephew, with one foot in the grave like that. Anyway, I wrote (with Gherkins's permission, naturally) to say we had the book and had been specially interested by something we found there, and would he be so obliging as to tell us something of its history. I also——'

'But what did you find in it?'

'I don't think we'll tell him yet, Gherkins, shall we? I like to keep policemen guessing. As I was saying, when you so rudely interrupted me, I also asked him whether he knew anything about his good nephew's offer to buy it back. His answer has just arrived. He says he knows of nothing specially interesting about the book. It has been in the library untold years, and the tearing out of the maps must have been done a long time ago by some family vandal. He can't think why his nephew should be so keen on it, as he certainly never pored over it as a boy. In fact, the old man declares the engaging Wilberforce has never even set foot in Yelsall Manor to his knowledge. So much for the fire-breathing monsters and the pleasant Sunday afternoons.'

'Naughty Wilberforce!'

'M'm. Yes. So, after last night's little dust-up, I wired the old boy we were tootling down to Yelsall to have a heart-to-heart talk with him about his picture-book and his nephew.'

'Are you taking the book down with you?' asked Parker. 'I can give you a police escort for it if you like.'

'That's not a bad idea,' said Wimsey. 'We don't know where the insinuating Mr. Pope may be hanging out, and I wouldn't put it past him to make another attempt.'

'Better be on the safe side,' said Parker. 'I can't come myself, but I'll send down a couple of men with you.'

'Good egg,' said Lord Peter. 'Call up your myrmidons. We'll get a car round at once. You're coming,

Gherkins, I suppose? God knows what your mother would say. Don't ever be an uncle, Charles; it's frightfully difficult to be fair to all parties.'

Yelsall Manor was one of those large, decaying country mansions which speak eloquently of times more spacious than our own. The original late Tudor construction had been masked by the addition of a wide frontage in the Italian manner, with a kind of classical portico surmounted by a pediment and approached by a semicircular flight of steps. The grounds had originally been laid out in that formal manner in which grove nods to grove and each half duly reflects the other. A late owner, however, had burst out into the more eccentric sort of landscape gardening which is associated with the name of Capability Brown. A Chinese pagoda, somewhat resembling Sir William Chambers's erection in Kew Gardens, but smaller, rose out of a grove of laurustinus towards the eastern extremity of the house, while at the rear appeared a large artificial lake, dotted with numerous islands, on which odd little temples, grottoes, teahouses, and bridges peeped out from among clumps of shrubs, once ornamental, but now sadly overgrown. A boat-house, with wide eaves like the designs on a willow-pattern plate, stood at one corner, its landing-stage fallen into decay and wreathed with melancholy weeds.

'My disreputable old ancestor, Cuthbert Conyers, settled down here when he retired from the sea in 1732,' said Dr. Conyers, smiling faintly. 'His elder brother died childless, so the black sheep returned to the fold with the determination to become respectable and found a family. I fear he did not succeed altogether. There were very queer tales as to where his money came from. He is said to have been a pirate, and to have sailed with the notorious Captain Blackbeard. In the village, to this day, he is remembered and spoken of as Cut-throat Conyers. It used to make the old man very angry, and there is an unpleasant story of his slicing the ears off a groom who had been heard to call him "Old Cut-throat". He was not an uncultivated person, though. It was he who did the landscape-gardening round at the back, and he built the pagoda for his telescope. He was reputed to study the Black Art, and there were certainly a number of astrological works in the library with his name on the fly-leaf, but probably the telescope was only a remembrance of his seafaring days.

'Anyhow, towards the end of his life he became more and more odd and morose. He quarrelled with his family, and turned his younger son out of doors with his wife and children. An unpleasant old fellow.

'On his deathbed he was attended by the parson—a good, earnest, God-fearing sort of man, who must have put up with a deal of insult in carrying out what he firmly believed to be the sacred duty of reconciling the old man to this shamefully treated son. Eventually, "Old Cut-throat" relented so far as to make a will, leaving to the younger son "My treasure which I have buried in Munster". The parson represented to him that it was useless to bequeath a treasure unless he also bequeathed the information where to find it, but the horrid old pirate only chuckled spitefully, and said that, as he had been at the pains to collect the treasure, his son might well be at the pains of looking for it. Further than that he would not go, and so he died, and I dare say went to a very bad place.

'Since then the family has died out, and I am the sole

representative of the Conyers, and heir to the treasure, whatever and wherever it is, for it was never discovered. I do not suppose it was very honestly come by, but, since it would be useless now to try and find the original owners, I imagine I have a better right to it than anybody living.

'You may think it very unseemly, Lord Peter, that an old, lonely man like myself should be greedy for a hoard of pirate's gold. But my whole life has been devoted to studying the disease of cancer, and I believe myself to be very close to a solution of one part at least of the terrible problem. Research costs money, and my limited means are very nearly exhausted. The property is mortgaged up to the hilt, and I do most urgently desire to complete my experiments before I die, and to leave a sufficient sum to found a clinic where the work can be carried on.

'During the last year I have made very great efforts to solve the mystery of "Old Cut-throat's" treasure. I have been able to leave much of my experimental work in the most capable hands of my assistant, Dr. Forbes, while I pursued my researches with the very slender clue I had to go upon. It was the more expensive and difficult that Cuthbert had left no indication in his will whether Münster in Germany or Munster in Ireland was the hiding-place of the treasure. My journeys and my search in both places cost money and brought me no farther on my quest. I returned, disheartened, in August, and found myself obliged to sell my library, in order to defray my expenses and obtain a little money with which to struggle on with my sadly delayed experiments.'

'Ah!' said Lord Peter. 'I begin to see light.'

The old physician looked at him inquiringly. They had finished tea, and were seated around the great fireplace in the study. Lord Peter's interested questions about the beautiful, dilapidated old house and estate had led the conversation naturally to Dr. Conyers's family, shelving for the time the problem of the *Cosmographia*, which lay on a table beside them.

'Everything you say fits into the puzzle,' went on Wimsey, 'and I think there's not the smallest doubt what Mr. Wilberforce Pope was after, though how he knew that you had the *Cosmographia* here I couldn't say.'

'When I disposed of the library, I sent him a catalogue,' said Dr. Conyers. 'As a relative, I thought he ought to have the right to buy anything he fancied. I can't think why he didn't secure the book then, instead of behaving in this most shocking fashion.'

Lord Peter hooted with laughter.

'Why, because he never tumbled to it till afterwards,' he said. 'And oh, dear, how wild he must have been! I forgive him everything. Although,' he added, 'I don't want to raise your hopes too high, sir, for, even when we've solved old Cuthbert's riddle, I don't know that we're very much nearer to the treasure.'

'To the *treasure*?'

'Well, now, sir. I want you first to look at this page, where there's a name scrawled in the margin. Our ancestors had an untidy way of signing their possessions higgledy-piggledy in margins instead of in a decent, Christian way in the fly-leaf. This is a handwriting of somewhere about Charles I's reign: "Jac: Coniers". I take it that goes to prove that the book was in the possession of your family at any rate as early as the first half of the seventeenth century, and has remained there ever since. Right. Now we turn to page 1099, where we find a description of the discoveries of Christopher Columbus.

It's headed, you see, by a kind of map, with some of Mr. Pope's monsters swimming about in it, and apparently representing the Canaries, or, as they used to be called, the Fortunate Isles. It doesn't look much more accurate than old maps usually are, but I take it the big island on the right is meant for Lanzarote, and the two nearest to it may be Teneriffe and Gran Canaria.'

'But what's that writing in the middle?'

'That's just the point. The writing is later than "Jac: Coniers's" signature; I should put it about 1700—but, of course, it may have been written a good deal later still. I mean, a man who was elderly in 1730 would still use the style of writing he adopted as a young man, especially if, like your ancestor the pirate, he had spent the early part of his life in outdoor pursuits and hadn't done much writing.'

'Do you mean to say, Uncle Peter,' broke in the viscount excitedly, 'that that's "Old Cut-throat's" writing?'

'I'd be ready to lay a sporting bet it is. Look here, sir, you've been scouring round Münster in Germany and Munster in Ireland—but how about good old Sebastian Munster here in the library at home?'

'God bless my soul! Is it possible?'

'It's pretty nearly certain, sir. Here's what he says, written, you see, round the head of that sort of sea-dragon:

Hic in capite draconis ardet perpetuo Sol.
Here the sun shines perpetually upon the Dragon's Head.

Rather doggy Latin—sea-dog Latin, you might say, in fact.'

'I'm afraid,' said Dr. Conyers, 'I must be very stupid, but I can't see where that leads us.'

'No; "Old Cut-throat" was rather clever. No doubt he thought that, if anybody read it, they'd think it was just an allusion to where it says, farther down, that "the

Liber V. 1099

DE NOVIS INSVLIS,

quomodo, quando, & per quem

illæ inuentæ sint.

CHristophorus Columbus natione Genuensis, cùm diu in aula regis Hispan' rum deuersatus fuisset, animum induxit, ut hactenus inaccessas orbis partes p agraret. Petiit propterea à rege ut uoto suo non deesset, futuris sibi & toti His

islands were called *Fortunatæ* because of the wonderful temperature of the air and the clemency of the skies". But the cunning old astrologer up in his pagoda had a meaning of his own. Here's a little book published in 1678—Middleton's *Practical Astrology*—just the sort of popular handbook an amateur like "Old Cut-throat" would use. Here you are: "If in your figure you find Jupiter or Venus or *Dragon's head*, you may be confident there is Treasure in the place supposed. . . . If you find *Sol* to be the Significator of the hidden Treasure, you may conclude there is Gold, or some jewels." You know, sir, I think we may conclude it.'

'Dear me!' said Dr. Conyers. 'I believe, indeed, you must be right. And I am ashamed to think that if anybody had suggested to me that it could ever be profitable to me to learn the terms of astrology, I should have replied in my vanity that my time was too valuable to waste on such foolishness. I am deeply indebted to you.'

'Yes,' said Gherkins, 'but where *is* the treasure, uncle?'

'That's just it,' said Lord Peter. 'The map is very vague; there is no latitude or longitude given; and the directions, such as they are, seem not even to refer to any spot on the islands, but to some place in the middle of the sea. Besides, it is nearly two hundred years since the treasure was hidden, and it may already have been found by somebody or other.'

Dr. Conyers stood up.

'I am an old man,' he said, 'but I still have some strength. If I can by any means get together the money for an expedition, I will not rest till I have made every possible effort to find the treasure and to endow my clinic.'

'Then, sir, I hope you'll let me give a hand to the good work,' said Lord Peter.

Dr. Conyers had invited his guests to stay the night, and, after the excited viscount had been packed off to bed, Wimsey and the old man sat late, consulting maps and diligently reading Munster's chapter '*De Novis Insulis*', in the hope of discovering some further clue. At length, however, they separated, and Lord Peter went upstairs, the book under his arm. He was restless, however, and, instead of going to bed, sat for a long time at his window, which looked out upon the lake. The moon, a few days past the full, was riding high among small, windy clouds, and picked out the sharp eaves of the Chinese tea-houses and the straggling tops of the unpruned shrubs. 'Old Cut-throat' and his landscape-gardening! Wimsey could have fancied that the old pirate was sitting now beside his telescope in the preposterous pagoda, chuckling over his riddling testament and counting the craters of the moon. 'If *Luna*, there is silver.' The water of the lake was silver enough; there was a great smooth path across it, broken by the sinister wedge of the boat-house, the black shadows of the islands, and, almost in the middle of the lake, a decayed fountain, a writhing Celestial dragon-shape, spiny-backed and ridiculous.

Wimsey rubbed his eyes. There was something strangely familiar about the lake; from moment to moment it assumed the queer unreality of a place which one recognizes without having ever known it. It was like one's first sight of the Leaning Tower of Pisa—too like its picture to be quite believable. Surely, thought Wimsey, he knew that elongated island on the right, shaped rather like a winged monster, with its two little clumps of buildings. And the island to the left of it, like the British Isles, but warped out of shape. And the third island, between the others, and nearer. The three formed a triangle, with the Chinese fountain in the centre, the moon shining steadily upon its dragon head. '*Hic in capite draconis ardet perpetuo*——'

Lord Peter sprang up with a loud exclamation, and flung open the door into the dressing-room. A small figure wrapped in an eiderdown hurriedly uncoiled itself from the window-seat.

'I'm sorry, Uncle Peter,' said Gherkins. 'I was so *dreadfully* wide awake, it wasn't any good staying in bed.'

'Come here,' said Lord Peter, 'and tell me if I'm mad or dreaming. Look out of the window and compare it with the map—Old Cut-throat's "New Islands". He made 'em, Gherkins; he put 'em here. Aren't they laid out just like the Canaries? Those three islands in a triangle, and the fourth down here in the corner? And the boat-house where the big ship is in the picture? And the dragon fountain where the dragon's head is? Well, my son, that's where your hidden treasure's gone to. Get your things on, Gherkins, and damn the time when all good little boys should be in bed! We're going for a row on the lake, if there's a tub in that boat-house that'll float.'

'Oh, Uncle Peter! This is a *real* adventure!'

'All right,' said Wimsey. 'Fifteen men on the dead man's chest, and all that! Yo-ho-ho, and a bottle of Johnny Walker! Pirate expedition fitted out in dead of night to seek hidden treasure and explore the Fortunate Isles! Come on, crew!'

Lord Peter hitched the leaky dinghy to the dragon's knobbly tail and climbed out carefully, for the base of the fountain was green and weedy.

'I'm afraid it's your job to sit there and bail, Gherkins,' he said. 'All the best captains bag the really interesting jobs for themselves. We'd better start with the head. If the old blighter said head, he probably meant it.' He passed an arm affectionately round the creature's neck for support, while he methodically pressed and pulled the various knobs and bumps of its anatomy. 'It seems beastly solid, but I'm sure there's a spring somewhere. You won't forget to bail, will you? I'd simply hate to turn round and find the boat gone. Pirate chief marooned on island and all that. Well, it isn't its back hair, anyhow. We'll try its eyes. I say, Gherkins, I'm sure I felt something move, only it's frightfully stiff. We might have thought to bring some oil. Never mind; it's dogged as does it. It's coming. It's coming. Booh! Pah!'

A fierce effort thrust the rusted knob inwards, releasing a huge spout of water into his face from the dragon's gaping throat. The fountain, dry for many years, soared rejoicingly heavenwards, drenching the treasure-hunters, and making rainbows in the moonlight.

'I suppose this is "Old Cut-throat's" idea of humour,' grumbled Wimsey, retreating cautiously round the dragon's neck. 'And now I can't turn it off again. Well, dash it all, let's try the other eye.'

He pressed for a few moments in vain. Then, with a grinding clang, the bronze wings of the monster clapped down to its sides, revealing a deep square hole, and the fountain ceased to play.

'Gherkins!' said Lord Peter, 'we've done it. (But don't neglect bailing on that account!) There's a box here. And it's beastly heavy. No; all right, I can manage. Gimme the boat-hook. Now I do hope the old sinner really did have a treasure. What a bore if it's only one of his little jokes. Never mind—hold the boat steady. There. Always remember, Gherkins, that you can make quite an effective crane with a boat-hook and a stout pair of braces. Got it? That's right. Now for home and beauty. . . . Hullo! what's all that?'

As he paddled the boat round, it was evident that something was happening down by the boat-house. Lights were moving about, and a sound of voices came across the lake.

'They think we're burglars, Gherkins. Always misunderstood. Give way, my hearties—

'A-roving, a-roving, since roving's been my ru-i-in,
I'll go no more a-roving with you, fair maid.'

'Is that you, my lord?' said a man's voice as they drew in to the boat-house.

'Why, it's our faithful sleuths!' cried his lordship. 'What's the excitement?'

'We found this fellow sneaking round the boat-house,' said the man from Scotland Yard. 'He says he's the old gentleman's nephew. Do you know him, my lord?'

'I rather fancy I do,' said Wimsey. 'Mr. Pope, I think. Good evening. Were you looking for anything? Not a treasure, by any chance? Because we've just found one. Oh! don't say that. *Maxima reverentia*, you know. Lord St. George is of tender years. And, by the way, thank you so much for sending your delightful friends to call on me last night. Oh, yes, Thompson, I'll charge him all right. You there, doctor? Splendid. Now, if anybody's got a spanner or anything handy, we'll have a look at Great-grandpapa Cuthbert. And if he turns out to be old iron, Mr. Pope, you'll have had an uncommonly good joke for your money.'

An iron bar was produced from the boat-house and thrust under the hasp of the chest. It creaked and burst.

Dr. Conyers knelt down tremulously and threw open the lid.

There was a little pause.

'The drinks are on you, Mr. Pope,' said Lord Peter. 'I think, doctor, it ought to be a jolly good hospital when it's finished.'

HUGH WALPOLE

Mr. Oddy

THIS may seem to many people an old-fashioned story; it is perhaps for that reason that I tell it. I can recover here, it may be, for myself something of the world that is already romantic, already beyond one's reach, already precious for the things that one might have got out of it and didn't.

London of but a few years before the war! What a commonplace to point out its difference from the London of to-day and to emphasize the tiny period of time that made that difference!

We were all young and hopeful then, we could all live on a shilling a year and think ourselves well off, we could all sit in front of the lumbering horse buses and chat confidentially with the omniscient driver, we could all see Dan Leno in Pantomime and watch Farren dance at the Empire, we could all rummage among those cobwebby streets at the back of the Strand where Aldwych now flaunts her shining bosom and imagine Pendennis and Warrington, Copperfield and Traddles cheek by jowl with ourselves, we could all wait in the shilling queue for hours to see Ellen Terry in *Captain Brassbound* and Forbes Robertson in *Hamlet*, we could all cross the street without fear of imminent death, and above all we could all sink ourselves into that untidy higgledy-piggledy smoky and beery and gas-lampy London gone utterly and for ever.

But I have no wish to be sentimental about it; there is a new London which is just as interesting to its new citizens as the old London was to myself. It is my age that is the matter; before the war one was so *very* young.

I like, though, to try and recapture that time, and so, as a simple way to do it, I seize upon a young man; Tommy Brown we will call him. I don't know where Tommy Brown may be now; that Tommy Brown who lived as I did in two very small rooms in Glebe Place, Chelsea, who enjoyed hugely the sparse but economical meals provided so elegantly by two charming ladies at 'The Good Intent' down by the river, that charming hostelry whence looking through the bow windows you could see the tubby barges go floating down the river and the thin outline of Whistler's Battersea Bridge, and in the small room itself were surrounded by who knows what geniuses in the lump, geniuses of Art and Letters, of the Stage and of the Law.

For Tommy Brown in those days life was Paradisal.

He had come boldly from Cambridge to throw himself upon London's friendly bosom; despite all warnings to the contrary he was certain that it would be friendly; how could it be otherwise to so charming, so brilliant, so unusually attractive a young man? For Tommy was conceited beyond all that his youth warranted, conceited indeed without any reason at all.

He had, it is true, secured the post of reviewer to one of the London daily papers; this seemed to him when he looked back in later years a kind of miracle, but at the time no miracle at all, simply a just appreciation of his extraordinary talents. There was also reposing in one of the publisher's offices at that moment the manuscript of a novel, a novel that appeared to him of astonishing brilliance, written in the purest English, sparkling with wit, tense with drama.

These things were fine and reassuring enough, but there was more than that; he felt in himself the power to rise to the greatest heights; he could not see how anything could stop him, it was his destiny.

This pride of his might have suffered some severe shocks were it not that he spent all of his time with other young gentlemen quite as conceited as himself. I have heard talk of the present young generation and its agreeable consciousness of its own merits, but I doubt if it is anything in comparison with that little group of fifteen years ago. After all, the war has intervened—however young we may be and however greatly we may pretend this is an unstable world and for the moment heroics have departed from it. But for Tommy Brown and his friends the future was theirs and nobody could prevent it. Something pathetic in that as one looks back.

Tommy was not really so unpleasant a youth as I have described him—to his elders he must have appeared a baby, and his vitality at least they could envy. After all, why check his confidence? Life would do that heavily enough in its own good time.

Tommy, although he had no money and no prospects, was already engaged to a young woman, Miss Alice Smith. Alice Smith was an artist sharing with a girl friend a Chelsea studio, and she was as certain of her future as Tommy was of his.

They had met at a little Chelsea dance, and two days after the meeting they were engaged. She had no parents who mattered, and no money to speak of, so that the engagement was the easiest thing in the world.

Tommy, who had been in love before many times, knew, as he told his friend Jack Robinson so often as to bore that gentleman severely, that this time at last he knew what love was. Alice ordered him about—with her at any rate his conceit fell away—she had read his novel and pronounced it old-fashioned, the severest criticism she could possibly have made, and she thought his reviews amateur. He suffered then a good deal in her company. When he was away from her he told himself and everybody else that her critical judgement was marvellous, her comprehension of all the Arts quite astounding, but he left her sometimes with a miserable suspicion that perhaps after all he was not going to do anything very wonderful and that he would have to work very hard indeed to rise to her astonishing standards.

It was in such a mood of wholesome depression that he came one beautiful spring April day from the A.B.C. shop where he had been giving his Alice luncheon, and found his way to an old bookshop on the river-side round the corner from Oakley Street. This shop was kept by a gentleman called Mr. Burdett Coutts, and the grand associations of his name gave him from the very first a sort of splendour.

It was one of those old shops of which there are, thank God, still many examples surviving in London, in which the room was so small and the books so many that to move a step was to imperil your safety. Books ran in thick, tight rows from floor to ceiling everywhere, were piled in stacks upon the ground, and hung in perilous heaps over chairs and window ledges.

Mr. Burdett Coutts himself, a very stout and grizzled old man enveloped always in a grey shawl, crouched behind his spectacles in a far corner and took apparently no interest in anything save that he would snap the price at you if you brought him a volume and timorously inquired. He was not one of those old booksellers dear to the heart of Anatole France and other great men who would love to discourse to you of the beauties of 'The Golden Ass', the possibility of Homer being a lady, or the virtues of the second Hyperion over the first. Not at all; he ate biscuits which stuck in his grizzly beard, and wrote perpetually in a large moth-eaten ledger which was supposed by his customers to contain all the secrets of the universe.

It was just because Mr. Coutts never interfered with you that Tommy Brown loved his shop so dearly. If he had a true genuine passion that went far deeper than all his little superficial vanities and egotisms, it was his passion for books—books of any kind.

He had at this time no fine taste—all was fish that came to his net. The bundles of Thackeray and Dickens, parts tied up carelessly in coarse string, the old broken-backed volumes of Radcliffe and Barham and Galt, the red and gold Colburn's novelists, all these were exciting to him, just as exciting as though they had been a first Gray's *Elegy* or an original *Robinson Crusoe.*

He had, too, a touching weakness for the piles of fresh and neglected modern novels that lay in their discarded heaps on the dusty floor; young though he was, he was old enough to realize the pathos of these so short a time ago fresh from the bursting presses, so eagerly cherished through months of anxious watching by their fond authors, so swiftly forgotten, dead almost before they were born.

So he browsed, moving like a panting puppy with inquisitive nose from stack to stack with a gesture of excitement, tumbling a whole racket of books about his head, looking then anxiously to see whether the old man would be angry with him, and realizing for the thousandth time that the old man never was.

It was on this day, then, rather sore from the arrogancies of his Alice, that he tried to restore his confidence among these friendly volumes. With a little thrill of excited pleasure he had just discovered a number of the volumes born of those romantic and tragedy-haunted Nineties. Here in little thin volumes were the stories of Crackanthorpe, the poems of Dowson, *The Keynotes* of George Egerton, *The Bishop's Dilemma* of Ella d'Arcy, *The Happy Hypocrite* of Max Beerbohm.

Had he only been wise enough to give there and then for that last whatever the old man had asked him for it he would have been fortunate indeed, but the pennies in his pocket were few—he was not yet a book collector, but rather that less expensive but more precious thing, a book adorer. He had the tiny volume in his hand, when he was aware that some one had entered the shop and was standing looking over his shoulder.

He turned slowly and saw some one who at first sight seemed vaguely familiar, so familiar that he was plunged into confusion at once by the sense that he ought to say 'How do you do?' but could not accurately place him. The gentleman also seemed to know him very well, for he said in a most friendly way, 'Ah, yes, the "Nineties", a very fruitful period.'

Tommy stammered something, put down the Max Beerbohm, moved a little, and pulled about him a sudden shower of volumes. The room was filled with the racket of their tumbling, and a cloud of dust thickened about them, creeping into eyes and mouth and nose.

'I'm terribly sorry,' Tommy stammered, and then, looking up, was sorry the more when he saw how extremely neat and tidy the gentleman was and how terribly the little accident must distress him.

Tommy's friend must have been between sixty and seventy years of age, nearer seventy perhaps than sixty, but his black hair was thick and strong and stood up *en brosse* from a magnificent broad forehead. Indeed, so fine was the forehead and the turn of the head that the face itself was a little disappointing, being so round and chubby and amiable as to be almost babyish. It was not a weak face, however, the eyes being large and fine and the chin strong and determined.

The figure of this gentleman was short and thick-set and inclined to stoutness; he had the body of a prize-fighter now resting on his laurels. He was very beautifully clothed in a black coat and waistcoat, pepper-and-salt trousers, and he stood leaning a little on a thick ebony cane, his legs planted apart, his whole attitude that of one who was accustomed to authority. He had the look of a magistrate, or even of a judge, and had his face been less kindly Tommy would have said good-day, nodded to Mr. Burdett Coutts, and departed, but that was a smile difficult to resist.

'Dear me,' the gentleman said, 'this is a very dusty shop. I have never been here before, but I gather by the way that you knock the books about that it's an old friend of yours.'

Tommy giggled in a silly fashion, shifted from foot to foot, and then, desiring to seem very wise and learned, proved himself only very young and foolish.

'The "Nineties" are becoming quite romantic,' he said in his most authoritative voice, 'now that we're getting a good distance from them.'

'Ah, you think so!' said the gentleman courteously;

'that's interesting. I'm getting to an age now, I'm afraid, when nothing seems romantic but one's own youth and, ah, dear me! that was a very long time ago.'

This was exactly the way that kindly old gentlemen were supposed to talk, and Tommy listened with becoming attention.

'In my young day,' his friend continued, 'George Eliot seemed to everybody a magnificent writer: a little heavy in hand for these days, I'm afraid. Now who is the God of your generation, if it isn't impertinent to inquire?'

Tommy shifted again from foot to foot. Who was the God of his generation? If the truth must be told, in Tommy's set there were no Gods, only young men who might be Gods if they lived long enough.

'Well,' said Tommy awkwardly, 'Hardy, of course—er—it's difficult to say, isn't it?'

'Very difficult,' said the gentleman.

There was a pause then, which Tommy concluded by hinting that he was afraid that he must move forward to a very important engagement.

'May I walk with you a little way?' asked the gentleman very courteously, 'such a very beautiful afternoon.'

Once outside in the beautiful afternoon air everything was much easier; Tommy regained his self-confidence, and soon was talking with his accustomed ease and freedom. There was nothing very alarming in his friend after all, he seemed so very eager to hear everything that Tommy had to say. He was strangely ignorant too; he seemed to be interested in the Arts, but to know very little about them; certain names that were to Tommy household words were to this gentleman quite unknown. Tommy began to be a little patronizing. They parted at the top of Oakley Street.

'I wonder if you'd mind,' the gentleman said, 'our meeting again? The fact is, that I have very little opportunity of making friends with your generation. There are so many things that you could tell me. I am afraid it may be tiresome for you to spend an hour or two with so ancient a duffer as myself, but it would be very kind of you.'

Tommy was nothing if not generous; he said that he would enjoy another meeting very much. Of course he was very busy and his spare hours were not many, but a walk another afternoon could surely be managed. They made an appointment, they exchanged names; the gentleman's name was Mr. Alfred Oddy.

That evening, in the middle of a hilarious Chelsea party, Tommy suddenly discovered to his surprise that it would please him very much to see Mr. Oddy walk in through the door.

Although it was a hilarious party Tommy was not very happy; for one thing, Spencer Russell, the novelist, was there and showed quite clearly that he didn't think Tommy very interesting. Tommy had been led up and introduced to him, had said one or two things that seemed to himself very striking, but Spencer Russell had turned his back almost at once and entered into eager conversation with somebody else.

This wasn't very pleasant, and then his own beloved Alice was behaving strangely; she seemed to have no eyes nor ears for any one in the room save Spencer Russell, and this was the stranger in that only a week or so before she had in public condemned Spencer Russell's novels, utterly and completely, stating that he was written out, had nothing to say, and was as good as dead. To-night, however, he was not dead at all, and Tommy had the agony of observing her edge her way into the group surrounding him and then listen to him not only as though he were the fount of all wisdom, but an Adonis as well, which last was absurd seeing that he was fat and unwieldy and bald on the top of his head.

After a while Tommy came up to her and suggested that they should go, and received then the shock of his life when she told him that he could go if he liked, but that he was not to bother her. And she told him this in a voice so loud that everybody heard and many people tittered.

He left in a fury and spent then a night that he imagined to be sleepless, although in truth he slept during most of it.

It was with an eagerness that surprised himself that he met Mr. Oddy on the second occasion. He had not seen Alice for two days. He did not intend to be the one to apologize first; besides, he had nothing to apologize for; and yet during these two days there was scarcely a moment that he had not to restrain himself from running round to her studio and making it up.

When he met Mr. Oddy at the corner of Oakley Street he was a very miserable young man. He was so miserable that in five minutes he was pouring out all his woes.

He told Mr. Oddy everything, of his youth, his wonderful promise, and the extraordinary lack of appreciation shown to him by his relatives, of the historical novels that he had written at the age of anything from ten to sixteen and found only the cook for an audience, of his going to Cambridge, and his extraordinary development there so that he became Editor of *The Lion*, that remarkable but very short-lived literary journal, and the President of *The Bats*, the most extraordinary Essay Club that Cambridge had ever known; of how, alas, he took only a third in History owing to the perverseness of examiners; and so on and so on, until he arrived in full flood at the whole history of his love for Alice, of her remarkable talents and beauty, but of her strange temper and arrogance and general feminine perverseness.

Mr. Oddy listened to it all in the kindest way. There's no knowing where they walked that afternoon; they crossed the bridge and adventured into Battersea Park, and finally had tea in a small shop smelling of stale buns and liquorice drops. It was only as they turned homewards that it occurred to Tommy that he had been talking during the whole afternoon. He had the grace to see that an apology was necessary.

'I beg your pardon, sir,' he said, flushing a little, 'I'm afraid I have bored you dreadfully. The fact is, that this last quarrel with Alice has upset me very badly. What would you do if you were in my position?'

Mr. Oddy sighed. 'The trouble is,' he said, 'that I realize only too clearly that I shall never be in your position again. My time for romance is over, or at least I get my romance now in other ways. It wasn't always so; there was a lady once beneath whose windows I stood night after night merely for the pleasure of seeing her candle outlined behind the blind.'

'And did she love you,' Tommy asked eagerly, 'as much as you loved her?'

'Nobody, my dear boy,' Mr. Oddy replied, 'loves you as much as you love them; either they love you more or they love you less. The first of these is often boring, the second always tragic. In the present case I should go and make it up; after all, happiness is always worth having, even at the sacrifice of one's pride. She seems to me a very charming young lady.'

'Oh, she is,' Tommy answered eagerly. 'I'll take your advice, I'll go this very evening; in fact, if you don't mind, I think it would be rather a good time to find her in now.'

Mr. Oddy smiled and agreed; they parted to meet another day.

On the third occasion of their meeting, which was only two days after the second, Tommy cared for his companion enough to wish to find out something about him.

His scene of reconciliation with his beautiful Alice had not been as satisfactory as he had hoped; she had forgiven him, indeed, but given him quite clearly to understand that she would stand none of his nonsense either now or hereafter. The satisfactory thing would have been for Tommy there and then to have left her, never to see her again; he would thus have preserved both his pride and his independence; but, alas, he was in love, terribly in love, and her indignation made her appear only the more magnificent.

And so on this third meeting with his friend he was quite humble and longing for affection.

And then his curiosity was stirred. Who was this handsome old gentleman, with his touching desire for Tommy's companionship? There was an air about him that seemed to suggest that he was some one of importance in his own world; beyond this there was an odd sense that Tommy knew him in some way, had seen him somewhere; so on this third occasion Tommy came out with his questions.

Who was he? Was he married? What was his profession, or was he perhaps retired now? And another question that Tommy would have liked to have asked, and had not the impertinence, was as to why this so late interest in the Arts and combined with this interest this so complete ignorance?

Mr. Oddy seemed to know a great deal about everything else, but in this one direction his questions were childish. He seemed never to have heard of the great Spencer Russell at all (which secretly gave Tommy immense satisfaction), and as for geniuses like Mumpus and Peter Arrogance and Samuel Bird, even when Tommy explained how truly great these men were, Mr. Oddy appeared but little impressed.

'Well, at least,' Tommy burst out indignantly, 'I suppose you've read something by Henry Galleon? Of course he's a back number now, at least he is not modern if you know what I mean, but then he's been writing for centuries. Why, his first book came out when Trollope and George Eliot were still alive. Of course, between ourselves I think *The Roads*, for instance, a pretty fine book, but you should hear Spencer Russell go for it.'

No, Mr. Oddy had never heard of Henry Galleon.

But there followed a most enchanting description by Mr. Oddy of his life when he was a young man and how he once heard Dickens give a reading of *A Christmas Carol*, of how he saw an old lady in a sedan chair at Brighton (she was cracked, of course, and even then a hundred years after her time, but still he had seen it), of how London in his young day was as dark and dirty at night as it had been in Pepys' time, of how crinolines when he was young were so large that it was one of the sights to see a lady getting into a cab, of how in the music-halls there was a chairman who used to sit on the stage with a table in front of him, ring a bell and drink out of a mug of beer, of how he heard Jean de Reszke in *Siegfried* and Ternina in *Tristan*, and of how he had been at the first night when Ellen Terry and Irving had delighted the world with *The Vicar of Wakefield.*

Yes, not only had Mr. Oddy seen and done all these things, but he related the events in so enchanting a way, drew such odd little pictures of such unexpected things and made that old London live so vividly, that at last Tommy burst out in a volley of genuine enthusiasm: 'Why, you ought to be a writer yourself! Why don't you write your reminiscences?'

But Mr. Oddy shook his head gently, there were too many reminiscences, every one was always reminiscing; who wanted to hear these old men talk?

At last when they parted Mr. Oddy had a request—one thing above all things that he would like would be to attend one of these evening gatherings with his young friend to hear these young men and women talk. He promised to sit very quietly in a corner—he wouldn't be in anybody's way.

Of course Tommy consented to take him; there would be one next week, a really good one; but in his heart of hearts he was a little shy. He was shy not only for himself but also for his friend.

During these weeks a strange and most unexpected affection had grown up in his heart for this old man; he really did like him immensely, he was so kind and gentle and considerate.

But he would be rather out of place with Spencer Russell and the others; he would probably say something foolish, and then the others would laugh. They were on the whole a rather ruthless set and were no respecters of persons.

However, the meeting was arranged; the evening

came and with it Mr. Oddy, looking just as he always did, quiet and gentle but rather impressive in some way or another. Tommy introduced him to his hostess, Miss Thelma Bennet, that well-known futuristic artist, and then carefully settled him down in a corner with Miss Bennet's aunt, an old lady who appeared occasionally on her niece's horizon but gave no trouble because she was stone deaf and cared only for knitting.

It was a lively evening; several of the brighter spirits were there, and there was a great deal of excellent talk about literature. Every writer over thirty was completely condemned save for those few remaining who had passed eighty years of age and ceased to produce.

Spencer Russell especially was at his best; reputations went down before his vigorous fist like ninepins. He was so scornful that his brilliance was, as Alice Smith everywhere proclaimed, 'simply withering'. Every one came in for his lash, and especially Henry Galleon. There had been some article in some ancient monthly written by some ancient idiot suggesting that there was still something to be said for Galleon and that he had rendered some service to English literature. How Russell pulled that article to pieces! He even found a volume of Galleon's among Miss Bennet's books, took it down from the shelf and read extracts aloud to the laughing derision of the assembled company.

Then an odd thing occurred. Tommy, who loved to be in the intellectual swim, nevertheless stood up and defended Galleon. He defended him rather feebly, it is true, speaking of him as though he were an old man ready for the almshouse who nevertheless deserved a little consideration and pity. He flushed as he spoke, and the scorn with which they greeted his defence altogether silenced him. It silenced him the more because Alice Smith was the most scornful of them all; she told him that he knew nothing and never would know anything, and she imitated his piping excited treble, and then every one joined in.

How he hated this to happen before Mr. Oddy! How humiliating after all the things that he had told his friend, the implications that he was generally considered to be one of England's most interesting young men, the implication above all that although she might be a little rough to him at times Alice really adored him and was his warmest admirer. She did not apparently adore him to-night, and when he went out at last with Mr. Oddy into the wintry, rain-driven street it was all he could do to keep back tears of rage and indignation.

Mr. Oddy had, however, apparently enjoyed himself. He put his hand for a minute on the boy's shoulder.

'Good night, my dear boy,' he said. 'I thought it very gallant of you to stand up for that older writer as you did: that needed courage. I wonder,' he went on, 'whether you would allow me to come and take tea with you one day—just our two selves. It would be a great pleasure for me.'

And then, having received Tommy's invitation, he vanished into the darkness.

On the day appointed, Mr. Oddy appeared punctually at Tommy's rooms. That was not a very grand house in Glebe Place where Tommy lived, and a very soiled and battered landlady let Mr. Oddy in. He stumbled up the dark staircase that smelt of all the cabbage and all the beef and all the mutton ever consumed by lodgers between these walls, up again two flights of stairs, until at last there was the weather-beaten door with Tommy's visiting-card nailed upon it. Inside was Tommy, a plate with little cakes, raspberry jam, and some very black-looking toast.

Mr. Oddy, however, was appreciative of everything; especially he looked at the books. 'Why,' he said, 'you've got quite a number of the novels of that man you defended the other evening. I wonder you're not ashamed to have them if they're so out of date.'

'To tell you the truth,' said Tommy, speaking freely now that he was in his own castle, 'I like Henry Galleon awfully. I'm afraid I pose a good deal when I'm with those other men; perhaps you've noticed it yourself. Of course Galleon is the greatest novelist we've got, with Hardy and Meredith, only he's getting old, and everything that's old is out of favour with our set.'

'Naturally,' said Mr. Oddy, quite approving, 'of course it is.'

'I have got a photograph of Galleon,' said Tommy. 'I cut it out of a publisher's advertisement, but it was taken years ago.'

He went to his table, searched for a little and produced a small photograph of a very fierce-looking gentleman with a black beard.

'Dear me,' said Mr. Oddy, 'he does look alarming!'

'Oh, that's ever so old,' said Tommy. 'I expect he's mild and soft now, but he's a great man all the same; I'd like to see Spencer Russell write anything as fine as *The Roads* or *The Pattern in the Carpet.*'

They sat down to tea very happy and greatly pleased with one another.

'I do wish,' said Tommy, 'that you'd tell me something about yourself; we're such friends now, and I don't know anything about you at all.'

'I'd rather you didn't,' said Mr. Oddy. 'You'd find it so uninteresting if you did; mystery's a great thing.'

'Yes,' said Tommy, 'I don't want to seem impertinent, and of course if you don't want to tell me anything you needn't, but—I know it sounds silly, but, you see, I like you most awfully. I haven't liked anybody so much for ever so long, except Alice, of course. I don't feel as though you were of another generation or anything; it's just as though we were the same age!'

Mr. Oddy was enchanted. He put his hand on the boy's for a moment and was going to say something, when they were interrupted by a knock on the door, and the terrible-looking landlady appeared in the room. She apologized, but the afternoon post had come and she thought the young gentleman would like to see his letters. He took them, was about to put them down without opening them, when suddenly he blushed. 'Oh, from Alice,' he said. 'Will you forgive me a moment?'

'Of course,' said Mr. Oddy.

The boy opened the letter and read it. It fell from his hand on to the table. He got up gropingly as though he could not see his way, and went to the window and stood there with his back to the room. There was a long silence.

'Not bad news, I hope,' said Mr. Oddy at last.

Tommy turned round. His face was grey and he was biting his lips. 'Yes,' he answered, 'she's—gone off.'

'Gone off?' said Mr. Oddy, rising from the table.

'Yes,' said Tommy, 'with Russell. They were married at a registry office this morning.'

He half turned round to the window, then put his hands as though he would shield himself from some blow, then crumpled up into a chair, his head falling between his arms on the table.

Mr. Oddy waited. At last he said: 'Oh, I'm sorry; that's dreadful for you!'

The boy struggled, trying to raise his head and speak, but the words would not come. Mr. Oddy went behind him and put his hands on his shoulders.

'You know,' he said, 'you mustn't mind me. Of course, I'll go if you like, but if you could think of me for a moment as your oldest friend, old enough to be your father, you know.'

Tommy clutched his sleeve, then, abandoning the struggle altogether, buried his head in Mr. Oddy's beautiful black waistcoat.

Later he poured his heart out. Alice was all that he had; he knew that he wasn't any good as a writer, he was a failure altogether; what he'd done he'd done for Alice, and now that she'd gone——

'Well, there's myself,' said Mr. Oddy. 'What I mean is that you're not without a friend; and as for writing, if you only write to please somebody else, that's no use; you've got to write because you can't help it. There are too many writers in the world already for you to dare to add to their number unless you're simply compelled to. But there—I'm preaching. If it's any comfort to you to know, I went through just this same experience myself once—the lady whose candle I watched behind the blind. If you cared to, would you come and have dinner with me to-night at my home? Only the two of us, you know; but don't if you'd rather be alone.'

Tommy, clutching Mr. Oddy's hand, said he would come.

About half-past seven that evening he had beaten up his pride. Even in the depth of his misery he saw that they would never have got on together, he and Alice.

He was quickly working himself into a fine state of hatred of the whole female race, and this helped him—he would be a bachelor all his days, a woman-hater; he would preserve a glorious independence. How much better this freedom than a houseful of children and a bagful of debts.

Only, as he walked to the address that Mr. Oddy had given him he held sharply away from him the memory of those hours that he had spent with Alice, those hours of their early friendship when the world had been so wonderful a place that it had seemed to be made entirely of golden sunlight. He felt that he was an old man indeed as he mounted the steps of Mr. Oddy's house.

It was a fine house in Eaton Square. Mr. Oddy must be rich. He rang the bell, and a door was opened by a footman. He asked for Mr. Oddy.

The footman hesitated a little, and then, smiling, said: 'Oh, yes, sir, will you come in?'

He left his coat in the fine hall, mounted a broad staircase, and then was shown into the finest library that he had ever seen. Books! Shelf upon shelf of books, and glorious books, editions de luxe and, as he could see with half an eye, rare first editions and those lovely bindings in white parchment and vellum that he so longed one day himself to possess. On the broad writing-table there was a large photograph of Meredith; it was signed in sprawling letters, 'George Meredith, 1887'. What could this mean? Mr. Oddy, who knew nothing about literature, had been given a photograph by George Meredith and had this wonderful library! He stared bewildered about him.

A door at the far end of the library opened and an elegant young man appeared. 'Mr. Galleon,' he said, 'will be with you in a moment. Won't you sit down?'

Mr. Galleon! Henry Galleon! Instantly he saw it, remembered with horrid confusion his own ridiculous conceited talk, the abusive nonsense of Russell and the rest. 'My God!' he whispered aloud, 'what he must be thinking!'

The door opened again and Mr. Oddy appeared. Tommy Brown, his face crimson, stammered: 'It was a shame—if I'd only known!' and then, trying to stand up for himself, 'but I had that photograph and there was the beard.'

Mr. Oddy laughed. 'The beard went long ago,' he said; 'I suppose it *was* a shame, but I was hemmed in here in my castle; I had to find out what you young people were like. I get tired of all this sometimes; nobody tells me the truth here. I have to go to you and your friends for that.'

So they went down to dinner together.

Yes, this is an old story. Its principal interest, perhaps, is that it's true. I was, you see, myself Tommy Brown.

H. G. WELLS

The Door in the Wall

§ I

ONE confidential evening, not three months ago, Lionel Wallace told me this story of the Door in the Wall. And at the time I thought that so far as he was concerned it was a true story.

He told it me with such a direct simplicity of conviction that I could not do otherwise than believe in him. But in the morning, in my own flat, I woke to a different atmosphere; and as I lay in bed and recalled the things he had told me, stripped of the glamour of his earnest slow voice, denuded of the focused, shaded table light, the shadowy atmosphere that wrapped about him and me, and the pleasant bright things, the dessert and glasses and napery of the dinner we had shared, making them for the time a bright little world quite cut off from everyday realities, I saw it all as frankly incredible. 'He was mystifying!' I said, and then: 'How well he did it! . . . It isn't quite the thing I should have expected him, of all people, to do well.'

Afterwards as I sat up in bed and sipped my morning tea, I found myself trying to account for the flavour of reality that perplexed me in his impossible reminiscences, by supposing they did in some way suggest, present, convey—I hardly know which word to use—experiences it was otherwise impossible to tell.

Well, I don't resort to that explanation now. I have got over my intervening doubts. I believe now, as I believed at the moment of telling, that Wallace did to the very best of his ability strip the truth of his secret for me. But whether he himself saw, or only thought he saw, whether he himself was the possessor of an inestimable privilege or the victim of a fantastic dream, I cannot pretend to guess. Even the facts of his death, which ended my doubts for ever, throw no light on that.

That much the reader must judge for himself.

I forget now what chance comment or criticism of mine moved so reticent a man to confide in me. He was, I think, defending himself against an imputation of slackness and unreliability I had made in relation to a great public movement, in which he had disappointed me. But he plunged suddenly. 'I have,' he said, 'a preoccupation——

'I know,' he went on, after a pause, 'I have been negligent. The fact is—it isn't a case of ghosts or apparitions—but—it's an odd thing to tell of, Redmond—I am haunted. I am haunted by something—that rather takes the light out of things, that fills me with longings . . .'

He paused, checked by that English shyness that so often overcomes us when we would speak of moving or grave or beautiful things. 'You were at Saint Althelstan's all through,' he said, and for a moment that seemed to me quite irrelevant. 'Well'—and he paused. Then very haltingly at first, but afterwards more easily, he began to tell of the thing that was hidden in his life, the haunting memory of a beauty and a happiness that filled his heart with insatiable longings, that made all the interests and spectacle of worldly life seem dull and tedious and vain to him.

Now that I have the clue to it, the thing seems written visibly in his face. I have a photograph in which that look of detachment has been caught and intensified. It reminds me of what a woman once said of him—a woman who had loved him greatly. 'Suddenly,' she said, 'the interest goes out of him. He forgets you. He doesn't care a rap for you—under his very nose . . .'

Yet the interest was not always out of him, and when he was holding his attention to a thing Wallace could contrive to be an extremely successful man. His career, indeed, is set with success. He left me behind him long ago; he soared up over my head, and cut a figure in the world that I couldn't cut—anyhow. He was still a year short of forty, and they say now that he would have been in office and very probably in the new Cabinet if he had lived. At school he always beat me without effort—as it were by nature. We were at school together at Saint Althelstan's College in West Kensington for almost all our school-time. He came into the school as my co-equal, but he left far above me, in a blaze of scholarships and brilliant performance. Yet I think I made a fair average running. And it was at school I heard first of the 'Door in the Wall'—that I was to hear of a second time only a month before his death.

To him at least the Door in the Wall was a real door, leading through a real wall to immortal realities. Of that I am now quite assured.

And it came into his life quite early, when he was a little fellow between five and six. I remember how, as he sat making his confession to me with a slow gravity, he reasoned and reckoned the date of it. 'There was,' he said, 'a crimson Virginia creeper in it—all one bright uniform crimson, in a clear amber sunshine against a white wall. That came into the impression somehow, though I don't clearly remember how, and there were horse-chestnut leaves upon the clean pavement outside the green door. They were blotched yellow and green, you know, not brown nor dirty, so that they must have been new fallen. I take it that means October. I look out for horse-chestnut leaves every year and I ought to know.

'If I'm right in that, I was about five years and four months old.'

He was, he said, rather a precocious little boy—he learned to talk at an abnormally early age, and he was so sane and 'old-fashioned', as people say, that he was permitted an amount of initiative that most children scarcely attain by seven or eight. His mother died when he was two, and he was under the less vigilant and authoritative care of a nursery governess. His father was a stern, preoccupied lawyer, who gave him little attention and expected great things of him. For all his brightness he found life grey and dull, I think. And one day he wandered.

He could not recall the particular neglect that enabled him to get away, nor the course he took among the West Kensington roads. All that had faded among the incurable blurs of memory. But the white wall and the green door stood out quite distinctly.

As his memory of that childish experience ran, he did at the very first sight of that door experience a peculiar emotion, an attraction, a desire to get to the door and open it and walk in. And at the same time he had the clearest conviction that either it was unwise or it was wrong of him—he could not tell which—to yield to this attraction. He insisted upon it as a curious thing that he knew from the very beginning—unless memory has played him the queerest trick—that the door was unfastened, and that he could go in as he chose.

I seem to see the figure of that little boy, drawn and repelled. And it was very clear in his mind, too, though why it should be so was never explained, that his father would be very angry if he went in through that door.

Wallace described all these moments of hesitation to me with the utmost particularity. He went right past the door, and then, with his hands in his pockets and making an infantile attempt to whistle, strolled right along beyond the end of the wall. There he recalls a number of mean dirty shops, and particularly that of a plumber and decorator with a dusty disorder of earthenware pipes, sheet lead, ball taps, pattern books of wall-paper, and tins of enamel. He stood pretending to examine these things, and *coveting*, passionately desiring, the green door.

Then, he said, he had a gust of emotion. He made a run for it, lest hesitation should grip him again; he went plump with outstretched hand through the green door and let it slam behind him. And so, in a trice, he came into the garden that has haunted all his life.

It was very difficult for Wallace to give me his full sense of that garden into which he came.

There was something in the very air of it that exhilarated, that gave one a sense of lightness and good happening and well-being; there was something in the sight of it that made all its colour clean and perfect and subtly luminous. In the instant of coming into it one was exquisitely glad—as only in rare moments, and when one is young and joyful one can be glad in this world. And everything was beautiful there. . . .

Wallace mused before he went on telling me. 'You see,' he said, with the doubtful inflexion of a man who pauses at incredible things, 'there were two great panthers there. . . . Yes, spotted panthers. And I was not afraid. There was a long wide path with marble-edged flower borders on either side, and these two huge velvety beasts were playing there with a ball. One looked up and came towards me, a little curious as it seemed. It came right up to me, rubbed its soft round ear very gently against the small hand I held out, and purred. It was, I tell you, an enchanted garden. I know. And the size? Oh! it stretched far and wide, this way and that. I believe there were hills far away. Heaven knows where West Kensington had suddenly got to. And somehow it was just like coming home.

'You know, in the very moment the door swung to behind me, I forgot the road with its fallen chestnut leaves, its cabs and tradesmen's carts, I forgot the sort of gravitational pull back to the discipline and obedience of home, I forgot all hesitations and fear, forgot discretion, forgot all the intimate realities of this life. I became in a moment a very glad and wonder-happy little boy—in another world. It was a world with a different quality, a warmer, more penetrating and mellower light, with a faint clear gladness in its air, and wisps of sun-touched cloud in the blueness of its sky. And before me ran this long wide path, invitingly, with weedless beds on either side, rich with untended flowers, and these two great panthers. I put my little hands fearlessly on their soft fur, and caressed their round ears and the sensitive corners under their ears, and played with them, and it was as though they welcomed me home. There was a keen sense of home-coming in my mind, and when presently a tall, fair girl appeared in the pathway and came to meet me, smiling, and said "Well?" to me, and lifted me and kissed me, and put me down and led me by the hand, there was no amazement, but only an impression of delightful rightness, of being reminded of happy things that had in some strange way been overlooked. There were broad red steps, I remember, that came into view between spikes of delphinium, and up these we went to a great avenue between very old and shady dark trees. All down this avenue, you know, between the red chapped stems, were marble seats of honour and statuary, and very tame and friendly white doves. . . .

'Along this cool avenue my girl-friend led me, looking down—I recall the pleasant lines, the finely modelled chin of her sweet kind face—asking me questions in a soft, agreeable voice, and telling me things, pleasant things I know, though what they were I was never able to recall. . . . Presently a Capuchin monkey, very clean, with a fur of ruddy brown and kindly hazel eyes, came down a tree to us and ran beside me, looking up at me and grinning, and presently leaped to my shoulder. So we two went on our way in great happiness.'

He paused.

'Go on,' I said.

'I remember little things. We passed an old man musing among laurels, I remember, and a place gay with paroquets, and came through a broad shaded colonnade to a spacious cool palace, full of pleasant fountains, full of beautiful things, full of the quality and promise of heart's desire. And there were many things and many people, some that still seem to stand out clearly and some that are vaguer; but all these people were beautiful and kind. In some way—I don't know how—it was conveyed to me that they all were kind to me, glad to have me there, and filling me with gladness by their gestures, by the touch of their hands, by the welcome and love in their eyes. Yes——'

He mused for a while. 'Playmates I found there. That was very much to me, because I was a lonely little boy. They played delightful games in a grass-covered court where there was a sun-dial set about with flowers. And as one played one loved. . . .

'But—it's odd—there's a gap in my memory. I don't remember the games we played. I never remembered. Afterwards, as a child, I spent long hours trying, even with tears, to recall the form of that happiness. I wanted to play it all over again—in my nursery—by myself. No! All I remember is the happiness and two dear playfellows who were most with me. . . . Then presently came a sombre dark woman, with a grave, pale face and dreamy eyes, a sombre woman, wearing a soft long robe of pale purple, who carried a book, and beckoned and took me aside with her into a gallery above a hall—though my playmates were loth to have me go, and ceased their game and stood watching as I was carried away. "Come back to us!" they cried. "Come back to us soon!" I looked up at her face, but she heeded them not at all. Her face was very gentle and grave. She took me to a seat in the gallery, and I stood beside her, ready to look at her book as she opened it upon her knee. The pages fell open. She pointed, and I looked, marvelling, for in the living pages of that book I saw myself; it was a story about myself, and in it were all the things that had happened to me since ever I was born. . . .

'It was wonderful to me, because the pages of that book were not pictures, you understand, but realities.'

Wallace paused gravely—looked at me doubtfully.

'Go on,' I said. 'I understand.'

'They were realities—yes, they must have been; people moved and things came and went in them; my dear mother, whom I had near forgotten; then my father, stern and upright, the servants, the nursery, all the familiar things of home. Then the front door and the busy streets, with traffic to and fro. I looked and marvelled, and looked half doubtfully again into the woman's face and turned the pages over, skipping this and that, to see more of this book and more, and so at last I came to myself hovering and hesitating outside the green door in the long white wall, and felt again the conflict and the fear.

' "And next?" I cried, and would have turned on, but the cool hand of the grave woman delayed me.

' "Next?" I insisted, and struggled gently with her hand, pulling up her fingers with all my childish strength, and as she yielded and the page came over she bent down upon me like a shadow and kissed my brow.

'But the page did not show the enchanted garden, nor the panthers, nor the girl who had led me by the hand, nor the playfellows who had been so loth to let me go. It showed a long grey street in West Kensington, in that chill hour of afternoon before the lamps are lit; and I was there, a wretched little figure, weeping aloud, for all that I could do to restrain myself, and I was weeping because I could not return to my dear playfellows who had called after me, "Come back to us! Come back to us soon!" I was there. This was no page in a book, but harsh reality; that enchanted place and the restraining hand of the grave mother at whose knee I stood had gone—whither had they gone?'

He halted again, and remained for a time staring into the fire.

'Oh! the woefulness of that return!' he murmured.

'Well?' I said, after a minute or so.

'Poor little wretch I was!—brought back to this grey world again! As I realized the fullness of what had happened to me, I gave way to quite ungovernable grief. And the shame and humiliation of that public weeping and my disgraceful home-coming remain with me still. I see again the benevolent-looking old gentleman in gold spectacles who stopped and spoke to me—prodding me first with his umbrella. "Poor little chap," said he; "and are you lost then?"—and me a London boy of five and more! And he must needs bring in a kindly young policeman and make a crowd of me, and so march me home. Sobbing, conspicuous, and frightened, I came back from the enchanted garden to the steps of my father's house.

'That is as well as I can remember my vision of that garden—the garden that haunts me still. Of course, I can convey nothing of that indescribable quality of translucent unreality, that *difference* from the common things of experience that hung about it all; but that—that is what happened. If it was a dream, I am sure it was a day-time and altogether extraordinary dream. . . . H'm!—naturally there followed a terrible questioning, by my aunt, my father, the nurse, the governess—every one. . . .

'I tried to tell them, and my father gave me my first thrashing for telling lies. When afterwards I tried to tell my aunt, she punished me again for my wicked persistence. Then, as I said, every one was forbidden to listen to me, to hear a word about it. Even my fairy-tale books were taken away from me for a time—because I was too "imaginative". Eh? Yes, they did that! My father belonged to the old school. . . . And my story was driven back upon myself. I whispered it to my pillow—my pillow that was often damp and salt to my whispering lips with childish tears. And I added always to my official and less fervent prayers this one heart-felt request: "Please God I may dream of the garden. Oh! take me back to my garden!" Take me back to my garden! I dreamt often of the garden. I may have added to it, I may have changed it; I do not know. . . . All this, you understand, is an attempt to reconstruct from fragmentary memories a very early experience. Between that and the other consecutive memories of my boyhood there is a gulf. A time came when it seemed impossible I should ever speak of that wonder glimpse again.'

I asked an obvious question.

'No,' he said. 'I don't remember that I ever attempted to find my way back to the garden in those early years. This seems odd to me now, but I think that very probably a closer watch was kept on my movements after this misadventure to prevent my going astray. No, it wasn't till you knew me that I tried for the garden again. And I believe there was a period—incredible as it seems now—when I forgot the garden altogether—when I was about eight or nine it may have been. Do you remember me as a kid at Saint Althelstan's?'

'Rather!'

'I didn't show any signs, did I, in those days of having a secret dream?'

§ 2

He looked up with a sudden smile.

'Did you ever play North-West Passage with me? . . . No, of course you didn't come my way!'

'It was the sort of game,' he went on, 'that every

imaginative child plays all day. The idea was the discovery of a North-West Passage to school. The way to school was plain enough; the game consisted in finding some way that wasn't plain, starting off ten minutes early in some almost hopeless direction, and working my way round through unaccustomed streets to my goal. And one day I got entangled among some rather low-class streets on the other side of Campden Hill, and I began to think that for once the game would be against me and that I should get to school late. I tried rather desperately a street that seemed a cul-de-sac, and found a passage at the end. I hurried through that with renewed hope. "I shall do it yet," I said, and passed a row of frowsy little shops that were inexplicably familiar to me, and behold! there was my long white wall and the green door that led to the enchanted garden!

'The thing whacked upon me suddenly. Then, after all, that garden, that wonderful garden, wasn't a dream!'

He paused.

'I suppose my second experience with the green door marks the world of difference there is between the busy life of a schoolboy and the infinite leisure of a child. Anyhow, this second time I didn't for a moment think of going in straight away. You see——. For one thing, my mind was full of the idea of getting to school in time—set on not breaking my record for punctuality. I must surely have felt *some* little desire at least to try the door—yes. I must have felt that. . . . But I seem to remember the attraction of the door mainly as another obstacle to my overmastering determination to get to school. I was immensely interested by this discovery I had made, of course—I went on with my mind full of it—but I went on. It didn't check me. I ran past, tugging out my watch, found I had ten minutes still to spare, and then I was going downhill into familiar surroundings. I got to school, breathless, it is true, and wet with perspiration, but in time. I can remember hanging up my coat and hat. . . . Went right by it and left it behind me. Odd, eh?'

He looked at me thoughtfully. 'Of course I didn't know then that it wouldn't always be there. Schoolboys have limited imaginations. I suppose I thought it was an awfully jolly thing to have it there, to know my way back to it; but there was the school tugging at me. I expect I was a good deal distraught and inattentive that morning, recalling what I could of the beautiful strange people I should presently see again. Oddly enough I had no doubt in my mind that they would be glad to see me. . . . Yes, I must have thought of the garden that morning just as a jolly sort of place to which one might resort in the interludes of a strenuous scholastic career.

'I didn't go that day at all. The next day was a half-holiday, and that may have weighed with me. Perhaps, too, my state of inattention brought down impositions upon me, and docked the margin of time necessary for the *détour*. I don't know. What I do know is that in the meantime the enchanted garden was so much upon my mind that I could not keep it to myself.

'I told—what was his name?—a ferrety-looking youngster we used to call Squiff.'

'Young Hopkins,' said I.

'Hopkins it was. I did not like telling him. I had a feeling that in some way it was against the rules to tell him, but I did. He was walking part of the way home with me; he was talkative, and if we had not talked about the enchanted garden we should have talked of something else, and it was intolerable to me to think about any other subject. So I blabbed.

'Well, he told my secret. The next day in the play interval I found myself surrounded by half a dozen bigger boys, half teasing, and wholly curious to hear more of the enchanted garden. There was that big Fawcett—you remember him?—and Carnaby and Morley Reynolds. You weren't there by any chance? No, I think I should have remembered if you were. . . .

'A boy is a creature of odd feelings. I was, I really believe, in spite of my secret self-disgust, a little flattered to have the attention of these big fellows. I remember particularly a moment of pleasure caused by the praise of Crawshaw—you remember Crawshaw major, the son of Crawshaw the composer?—who said it was the best lie he had ever heard. But at the same time there was a really painful undertow of shame at telling what I felt was indeed a sacred secret. That beast Fawcett made a joke about the girl in green——'

Wallace's voice sank with the keen memory of that shame. 'I pretended not to hear,' he said. 'Well, then Carnaby suddenly called me a young liar, and disputed with me when I said the thing was true. I said I knew where to find the green door, could lead them all there in ten minutes. Carnaby became outrageously virtuous, and said I'd have to—and bear out my words or suffer. Did you ever have Carnaby twist your arm? Then perhaps you'll understand how it went with me. I swore my story was true. There was nobody in the school then to save a chap from Carnaby, though Crawshaw put in a word or so. Carnaby had got his game. I grew excited and red-eared, and a little frightened. I behaved altogether like a silly little chap, and the outcome of it all was that instead of starting alone for my enchanted garden, I led the way presently—cheeks flushed, ears hot, eyes smarting, and my soul one burning misery and shame—for a party of six mocking, curious, and threatening schoolfellows.

'We never found the white wall and the green door....'

'You mean——?'

'I mean I couldn't find it. I would have found it if I could.

'And afterwards when I could go alone I couldn't find it. I never found it. I seem now to have been always looking for it through my schoolboy days, but I never came upon it—never.'

'Did the fellows—make it disagreeable?'

'Beastly. . . . Carnaby held a council over me for wanton lying. I remember how I sneaked home and upstairs to hide the marks of my blubbering. But when I cried myself to sleep at last it wasn't for Carnaby, but for the garden, for the beautiful afternoon I had hoped for, for the sweet friendly women and the waiting playfellows, and the game I had hoped to learn again, that beautiful forgotten game. . . .

'I believed firmly that if I had not told—— . . . I had bad times after that—crying at night and wool-gathering by day. For two terms I slacked and had bad reports. Do you remember? Of course you would! It was *you*—your beating me in mathematics that brought me back to the grind again.'

§ 3

For a time my friend stared silently into the red heart of the fire. Then he said: 'I never saw it again until I was seventeen.

'It leaped upon me for the third time—as I was driving to Paddington on my way to Oxford and a scholarship. I had just one momentary glimpse. I was leaning over the apron of my hansom smoking a cigarette, and no doubt thinking myself no end of a man of the world, and suddenly there was the door, the wall, the dear sense of unforgettable and still attainable things.

'We clattered by—I too taken by surprise to stop my cab until we were well past and round a corner. Then I had a queer moment, a double and divergent movement of my will: I tapped the little door in the roof of the cab, and brought my arm down to pull out my watch. "Yes, sir!" said the cabman, smartly. "Er—well—it's nothing," I cried. "*My* mistake! We haven't much time! Go on!" And he went on. . . .

'I got my scholarship. And the night after I was told of that I sat over my fire in my little upper room, my study, in my father's house, with his praise—his rare praise—and his sound counsels ringing in my ears, and I smoked my favourite pipe—the formidable bulldog of adolescence—and thought of that door in the long white wall. "If I had stopped," I thought, "I should have missed my scholarship, I should have missed Oxford—muddled all the fine career before me! I begin to see things better!" I fell musing deeply, but I did not doubt then this career of mine was a thing that merited sacrifice.

'Those dear friends and that clear atmosphere seemed very sweet to me, very fine but remote. My grip was fixing now upon the world. I saw another door opening—the door of my career.'

He stared again into the fire. Its red light picked out a stubborn strength in his face for just one flickering moment, and then it vanished again.

'Well,' he said and sighed, 'I have served that career. I have done—much work, much hard work. But I have dreamt of the enchanted garden a thousand dreams, and seen its door, or at least glimpsed its door, four times since then. Yes—four times. For a while this world was so bright and interesting, seemed so full of meaning and opportunity, that the half-effaced charm of the garden was by comparison gentle and remote. Who wants to pat panthers on the way to dinner with pretty women and distinguished men? I came down to London from Oxford, a man of bold promise that I have done something to redeem. Something—and yet there have been disappointments. . . .

'Twice I have been in love—I will not dwell on that—but once, as I went to some one who, I knew, doubted whether I dared to come, I took a short cut at a venture through an unfrequented road near Earl's Court, and so happened on a white wall and a familiar green door. "Odd!" said I to myself, "but I thought this place was on Campden Hill. It's the place I never could find somehow—like counting Stonehenge—the place of that queer daydream of mine." And I went by it intent upon my purpose. It had no appeal to me that afternoon.

'I had just a moment's impulse to try the door, three steps aside were needed at the most—though I was sure enough in my heart that it would open to me—and then I thought that doing so might delay me on the way to that appointment in which my honour was involved. Afterwards I was sorry for my punctuality—I might at least have peeped in and waved a hand to those panthers, but I knew enough by this time not to seek again belatedly that which is not found by seeking. Yes, that time made me very sorry. . . .

'Years of hard work after that, and never a sight oı the door. It's only recently it has come back to me. With it there has come a sense as though some thin tarnish had spread itself over my world. I began to think of it as a sorrowful and bitter thing that I should never see that door again. Perhaps I was suffering a little from overwork—perhaps it was what I've heard spoken of as the feeling of forty. I don't know. But certainly the keen brightness that makes effort easy has gone out of things recently, and that just at a time—with all these new political developments—when I ought to be working. Odd, isn't it? But I do begin to find life toilsome, its rewards, as I come near them, cheap. I began a little while ago to want the garden quite badly. Yes—and I've seen it three times.'

'The garden?'

'No—the door! And I haven't gone in!'

He leaned over the table to me, with an enormous sorrow in his voice as he spoke. 'Thrice I have had my chance—*thrice!* If ever that door offers itself to me again, I swore, I will go in, out of this dust and heat, out of this dry glitter of vanity, out of these toilsome futilities. I will go and never return. This time I will stay. . . . I swore it, and when the time came—*I didn't go.*

'Three times in one year have I passed that door and failed to enter. Three times in the last year.

'The first time was on the night of the snatch division on the Tenants' Redemption Bill, on which the Government was saved by a majority of three. You remember? No one on our side—perhaps very few on the opposite side—expected the end that night. Then the debate collapsed like eggshells. I and Hotchkiss were dining with his cousin at Brentford; we were both unpaired, and we were called up by telephone, and set off at once in his cousin's motor. We got in barely in time, and on the way we passed my wall and door—livid in the moonlight, blotched with hot yellow as the glare of our lamps lit it, but unmistakable. "My God!" cried I. "What?" said Hotchkiss. "Nothing!" I answered, and the moment passed.

' "I've made a great sacrifice," I told the whip as I got in. "They all have," he said, and hurried by.

'I do not see how I could have done otherwise then. And the next occasion was as I rushed to my father's bedside to bid that stern old man farewell. Then, too, the claims of life were imperative. But the third time was different; it happened a week ago. It fills me with hot remorse to recall it. I was with Gurker and Ralphs—it's no secret now, you know, that I've had my talk with Gurker. We had been dining at Frobisher's, and the talk had become intimate between us. The question of my place in the reconstructed Ministry lay always just over the boundary of the discussion. Yes—yes. That's all settled. It needn't be talked about yet, but there's no reason to keep a secret from you. . . . Yes—thanks! thanks! But let me tell you my story.

'Then, on that night things were very much in the air. My position was a very delicate one. I was keenly anxious to get some definite word from Gurker, but was hampered by Ralphs' presence. I was using the best power of my brain to keep that light and careless talk not too obviously directed to the point that concerned me. I had to. Ralphs' behaviour since has more than justified my caution. . . . Ralphs, I knew, would leave us beyond the Kensington High Street, and then I could surprise Gurker by a sudden frankness. One has sometimes to resort to these little devices. . . . And then it was that in the margin of my field of vision I became aware once more of the white wall, the green door before us down the road.

'We passed it talking. I passed it. I can still see the shadow of Gurker's marked profile, his opera hat tilted forward over his prominent nose, the many folds of his neck wrap going before my shadow and Ralphs' as we sauntered past.

'I passed within twenty inches of the door. "If I say good-night to them, and go in," I asked myself, "what will happen?" And I was all a-tingle for that word with Gurker.

'I could not answer that question in the tangle of my other problems. "They will think me mad," I thought. "And suppose I vanish now!—Amazing disappearance of a prominent politician!" That weighed with me. A thousand inconceivably petty worldlinesses weighed with me in that crisis.'

Then he turned on me with a sorrowful smile, and, speaking slowly, 'Here I am!' he said.

'Here I am!' he repeated, 'and my chance has gone from me. Three times in one year the door has been offered me—the door that goes into peace, into delight, into a beauty beyond dreaming, a kindness no man on earth can know. And I have rejected it, Redmond, and it has gone——'

'How do you know?'

'I know. I know. I am left now to work it out, to stick to the tasks that held me so strongly when my moments came. You say I have success—this vulgar, tawdry, irksome, envied thing. I have it.' He had a walnut in his big hand. 'If that was my success,' he said, and crushed it, and held it out for me to see.

'Let me tell you something, Redmond. This loss is destroying me. For two months, for ten weeks nearly now, I have done no work at all, except the most necessary and urgent duties. My soul is full of inappeasable regrets. At nights—when it is less likely I shall be recognized—I go out. I wander. Yes. I wonder what people would think of that if they knew. A Cabinet Minister, the responsible head of that most vital of all departments, wandering alone—grieving—sometimes near audibly lamenting—for a door, for a garden!'

§ 4

I can see now his rather pallid face, and the unfamiliar sombre fire that had come into his eyes. I see him very vividly to-night. I sit recalling his words, his tones, and last evening's *Westminster Gazette* still lies on my sofa, containing the notice of his death. At lunch to-day the club was busy with his death. We talked of nothing else.

They found his body very early yesterday morning in a deep excavation near East Kensington Station. It is one of two shafts that have been made in connexion with an extension of the railway southward. It is protected from the intrusion of the public by a hoarding upon the high road, in which a small doorway has been cut for the convenience of some of the workmen who live in that direction. The doorway was left unfastened through a misunderstanding between two gangers, and through it he made his way.

My mind is darkened with questions and riddles.

It would seem he walked all the way from the House that night—he has frequently walked home during the past Session—and so it is I figure his dark form coming along the late and empty streets, wrapped up, intent. And then did the pale electric lights near the station cheat the rough planking into a semblance of white? Did that fatal unfastened door awaken some memory?

Was there, after all, ever any green door in the wall at all?

I do not know. I have told his story as he told it to me. There are times when I believe that Wallace was no more than the victim of the coincidence between a rare but not unprecedented type of hallucination and a careless trap, but that indeed is not my profoundest belief. You may think me superstitious, if you will, and foolish; but, indeed, I am more than half convinced that he had, in truth, an abnormal gift, and a sense, something—I know not what—that in the guise of wall and door offered him an outlet, a secret and peculiar passage of escape into another and altogether more beautiful world. At any rate, you will say, it betrayed him in the end. But did it betray him? There you touch the inmost mystery of these dreamers, these men of vision and the imagination. We see our world fair and common, the hoarding and the pit. By our daylight standard he walked out of security into darkness, danger, and death.

But did he see like that?

BIOGRAPHICAL NOTES

BENSON, STELLA (1892–1933). Educated at home. Life largely spent abroad in Switzerland, France, Germany, America, and China. Took a small part in Women Suffrage work 1914. During the War worked for eighteen months in East London, later on the land. Went to America 1918, and lived chiefly in California until 1920. Her published works include: *I Pose*; *This is the End*; *Living Alone*; *The Poor Man*; *The Little World, Sketches of Travel*; *Worlds within Worlds*; *Tobit Transplanted,* and *Hope against Hope.*

GALSWORTHY, JOHN (1869–1933). O.M. (1929). Educated at Harrow, and New College, Oxford. Travelled very extensively. Wrote a great number of novels, plays, and short stories, including the series beginning with *The Man of Property*; *The Silver Box*; *Strife*; *Justice*; *The Inn of Tranquillity*; *The Skin Game*; *The Forsyte Saga*; *Loyalties*; *The Forest*; *Maid in Waiting*, and *Flowering Wilderness.*

HUGHES, RICHARD (1900–1976). Educated at Charterhouse, and Oriel College, Oxford. Author and dramatist; contributor to London and American literary journals; co-founder of the Portmadoc Players; Vice-Chairman of the Welsh National Theatre. His published works include: *The Sisters' Tragedy*; *A Comedy of Good and Evil*; *A Moment of Time*; *A High Wind in Jamaica*; *The Spider's Palace*, and *In Hazard.*

JAMES, MONTAGUE RHODES (1862–1936). O.M., Litt.D. Born at Livermere, Suffolk. Educated at Eton, and King's College, Cambridge. Bell Scholar; Craven Scholar; 1st Chancellor's Medallist; Director of Fitzwilliam Museum; Provost of King's College, Cambridge; Schweich Lecturer, British Academy; David Murray Lecturer, Glasgow University, and Provost of Eton. His published works include: *Psalms of Solomon* and *Testament of Abraham.* His writings are very numerous, including much editorial work on ancient MSS. and on stained glass. His works include also: *Ghost Stories of an Antiquary*; *More Ghost Stories of an Antiquary*;

A Thin Ghost and Others; *The Five Jars*; *A Warning to the Curious*, and *Collected Ghost Stories*.

MAUGHAM, WILLIAM SOMERSET (1874–1965). F.R.S.L., M.R.C.S., L.R.C.P. Educated at King's School, Canterbury, Heidelberg University, and St. Thomas's Hospital. Author and dramatist; Officer of the Legion of Honour. His published works include: *Liza of Lambeth*; *Mrs. Craddock*; *The Merry-go-round*; *The Bishop's Apron*; *The Explorer*; *The Magician*; *The Moon and Sixpence*; *The Trembling of a Leaf*; *The Painted Veil*; *Ashenden*; *Cakes and Ale*; and the following plays: *A Man of Honour*; *Lady Frederick*; *Jack Straw*; *Penelope*; *Smith*; *Loaves and Fishes*; *The Land of Promise*; *Love in a Cottage*; *Our Betters*; *East of Suez*; *The Constant Wife*, and *The Breadwinner*.

MERRICK, LEONARD (1864–1939). Born in London. Educated at Brighton College and private schools. His published works include: *A Chair on the Boulevard*; *Conrad in Quest of his Youth*; *When Love Flies out o' the Window*; *The Position of Peggy Harper*; *The Man who Understood Women*; *The Quaint Companions*; *Cynthia*; *One Man's View*; *The Worldlings*; *The Actor-Manager*; *While Paris Laughed*, and *A Woman in the Case*. His work was reissued in 1918 in a collected edition with Introductions by some of the most famous writers of the day.

MITCHISON, NAOMI MARGARET (1897). Born in Edinburgh. Educated at the Dragon School, Oxford, and Oxford University (Home Student). Officier de l'Académie Française; Labour Candidate for Scottish Universities, 1935. Her published works include: *The Conquered*; *Cloud Cuckoo Land*; *Black Sparta*; *Anna Comnena*; *Barbarian Stories*; *The Hostages*; *The Corn King and the Spring Queen*; *An Outline for Boys and Girls and Their Parents*; *The Home*; *We Have Been Warned*, and *The Fourth Pig*. Contributor to *New Statesman*, *Daily Herald*, *Clarion*, and *Time and Tide*.

MOSS, GEOFFREY (MAJOR G. MCNEILL-MOSS) (1888). Born in London. Educated at Rugby and R.M.C. Sandhurst. 2nd-Lieut. Grenadier Guards 1905–19; commanded a Battalion of the Gordon Highlanders in France 1915. His published works include: novels: *I face the Stars*; *Thursby*; *Sweet Pepper*; modern history: *The Epic of the Alcazar*, 1937; plays: *Sweet Pepper*; *The Siege*; short stories: *Defeat*; *The Three Cousins*, and *Wet Afternoon*.

'SAKI': MUNRO, HECTOR HUGH (1870–1916). Born in Burma. Educated at a private school at Exmouth, and later at Bedford. With his elder brother and his sister produced a newspaper. Lived in Normandy and Dresden. Settled in north Devon, and visited Davos. Joined the Burmese Mounted Police, and after having fever seven times returned to England. His literary talent was recognized by Sir Francis Gould, and he began to write for the *Westminster Gazette* under the name of 'Saki'. In 1902 he went to the Balkans for the *Morning Post* as journalist. In 1905 was correspondent for the *Morning Post* in St. Petersburg, and afterwards in Paris, returning to London in 1908. With great difficulty managed to enlist in the 2nd King Edward's Horse as a trooper, and later exchanged into the 22nd Royal Fusiliers, and rose to the rank of Lance-sergeant, having refused to take a commission. Fell in action at Beaumont-Hamel in 1916. His published works include: *The Chronicles of Clovis*; *The Unbearable Bassington*; *When William Came*, and *The Toys of Peace*.

O'CONNOR, FRANK (1903–1966). Born in Cork. Educated by the Christian Brothers. His published works include: *Guests of the Nation* and *Bones of Contention* (stories); *The Saint and Mary Kate* (novel); *The Wild Birds' Nest* and *Lords and Commons* (verse), and *The Big Fellow* (biography).

SAYERS, DOROTHY LEIGH (MRS. FLEMING) (1893–1957). Educated at Somerville College, Oxford. Her published works include: *Clouds of Witness*; *Unnatural Death*; *The Unpleasantness at the Bellona Club*; *Lord Peter views the Body*; *Strong Poison*; *Murder Must Advertise*; *The Nine Tailors*; *Gaudy Night*; *Busman's Honeymoon* (also a play with M. St. Clare Byrne), and *The Zeal of Thy House*. Edited *Great Short Stories of Detection, Mystery and Horror*.

WALPOLE, SIR HUGH SEYMOUR (1884–1941). Born in Edinburgh. Educated at King's School, Canterbury, and Emmanuel College, Cambridge. Served with the Russian Red Cross in European War. His published works include: *Mr. Perrin and Mr. Trail*; *Fortitude*; *The Dark Forest*; *The Green Mirror*; *The Secret City*; *The Captives*; *The Cathedral*; *The Old Ladies*; *Portrait of a Man with Red Hair*, and *Harmer John*. He gave the Rede Lecture on the English Novel in 1925.

WELLS, HERBERT GEORGE (1866–1946). Educated at Midhurst Grammar School, and the Royal College of Science, from which he graduated with first-class honours in Zoology. After teaching Science for some time he took to journalism, and since then devoted himself to writing. The books themselves are so numerous that only the more important can be mentioned. His first efforts in fiction took the form of scientific romances: *The Time Machine*; *The Stolen Bacillus*; *The Invisible Man*; *The Plattner Story*; *The War of the Worlds*; *Tales of Space and Time*, and *The Food of the Gods*; then came a series of genuine novels: *Love and Mr. Lewisham*; *Kipps*, and *The History of Mr. Polly*; after this a series introducing problems of modern society, social, religious, political, and commercial: *Mankind in the Making*; *Tono-Bungay*; *Ann Veronica*; *The New Machiavelli*; *Marriage*; *The World of William Clissold*; and a fourth series with the discursive and dogmatic elements predominant: *Mr. Britling Sees It Through* and *Joan and Peter*. In addition the following should be mentioned: *The Island of Doctor Moreau*; *A Modern Utopia*; *New Worlds for Old*; *The Outline of History*; *A Short History of the World*, and a study of modern educational methods in *The Story of a Great Schoolmaster*; *The Open Conspiracy*; *The Work, Wealth, and Happiness of Mankind*; *The Shape of Things to Come*, and *Experiment in Autobiography*.

ACKNOWLEDGEMENTS

We are grateful for permission to reproduce the following copyright stories.

Richard Hughes: 'A Night at a Cottage'. Reprinted by permission of David Higham Associates Ltd.

W. Somerset Maugham: 'Jane' from *Complete Short Stories*. Reprinted by permission of William Heinemann Ltd., and A. P. Watt Ltd, on behalf of the Royal Literary Fund.

Leonard Merrick: 'Judgement of Paris'. Reprinted by permision of the National Society for Cancer Relief.

Naomi Mitchison: 'The Hostages'. Reprinted by permission of David Higham Associates Ltd.

Frank O'Connor: 'The Majesty of the Law'. Copyright 1952 by Frank O'Connor. Reprinted from *Collected Stories* by Frank O'Connor, by permission of Alfred A. Knopf, Inc. and from *Stories of Frank O'Connor* (Hamish Hamilton Ltd.) by permission of A. D. Peters & Co. Ltd.

Dorothy L. Sayers: 'The Learned Adventure of the Dragon's Head' from *Lord Peter Wimsey Views the Body* (NEL). Reprinted by permission of David Higham Associates Ltd.

Sir Hugh Walpole: 'Mr. Oddy'. Reprinted by permission of Sir Rupert Hart-Davis.

H. G. Wells: 'The Door In The Wall' from *The Short Stories of H. G. Wells*. Reprinted by permission of A. P. Watt Ltd., on behalf of The Literary Executors of the Estate of H. G. Wells.

Unfortunately we were unable to trace the copyright holder for the following. If contacted we shall be pleased to include correct acknowledgement in any future reprints and/or new editions:

Geoffrey McNeill Moss: 'Defeat' from *Defeat* (Century Hutchinson).